Tactical Knives ■ **Dietmar Pohl**

In memory of
Jimmy Lile and Rex Applegate

Tactical
Knives

Development ■ **Areas of application** ■ **Models and manufacturers**

Dietmar Pohl

U.S. Edition copyright 2003 by Motorbuch Verlag

First published in Germany in 2001 by Motorbuch Verlag,
Postfach 103743, 70032 Stuttgart

Published by

krause publications
An F&W Publications Company

700 East State Street • Iola, WI 54990-0001
715-445-2214 • 888-457-2873
www.krause.com

Our toll-free number to place an order or obtain a free catalog is 800-258-0929.

Library of Congress Catalog Number: 2003105290

ISBN: 0-87349-636-1

Cover design: Katja Draenert using photos by Thomas Ruhl.

Pictures: Dietmar Pohl (unless otherwise indicated).

Table of Contents

Foreword by Conrad "Ben" Baker   7

Introduction   9

What Characterizes a Tactical Knife?   13

Combat knives of WWI and WWII   15
Influences and developments during the Vietnam War   22
■ *Conrad "Ben" Baker and the secret knives of the MACV/SOG*   28
■ *Randall Made 8Knives in Vietnam*   36
New trends in knives in the early 1980s   40
Developments by close-range combat specialist Rex Applegate   45

Knives in Tactical Deployment   55

Commando Special Forces (*Kommando Spezialkräfte*)   61
Border Protection Squadron 9 (*Grenzschutzgruppe 9*)   64
Police special forces (*Spezialeinsatzkommandos & Mobilen
Einsatzkommandos*)   68
Customs Central Support (*Zentrale Unterstützungsgruppe Zoll*)   73

Folding Tactical Knives   77

One-handed knives   81
Switchblade knives   85

Fixed-blade Tactical Knives   91

General-purpose knives   93
Maritime knives   97
Survival knives   103
Hatchet knives and field knives   108
Concealed knives   112

Tactical Specialized or Auxiliary Functions

117

Handle: Design Aspects and Materials

127

Forms   128
Handle materials   130
Hilts, pommels and thumb supports   139

Blades and Their Importance in Tactical Deployment

143

Shapes, geometries and styles   144
Blade materials   149
Serrated edges and teeth   158
Types of surface treatments   160

Tactical Carrying Possibilities and Systems

165

Folding knives   171
Fixed-blade knives   173
Optional sheaths and carrying accessories 176

Multifunctional Tools in Tactical Deployment

179

Appendix

Special Report: Got Game? Go Tactical   184
Final thoughts   189
About the author   190
Essential Internet sites devoted to tactical knives and accessories 191

Foreword

By Conrad "Ben" Baker

I t is truly an honor and a privilege to be asked to write the foreword to Dietmar Pohl's history of the evolution of the tactical knife from its roots at the turn of the 20th century, through both world wars, the Korean War and the Vietnam War, up to the present. My own minor contribution to the development of modern combat knives began in 1963, when I was appointed acting head of the U.S. Counter-Insurgency Support Office (CISO). Up to that point in time I had worked in Japan and Korea at the 34th RCT headquarters, as well as more than 16 years in the Army Engineer Corps. The only knives that I had ever seen at that time were utility knives, knives for cutting parachutes, KA-BAR knives and various bayonets.

CISO took over the support of paramilitary Special Forces operations in Vietnam from the CIA under a (then top-secret) program called "Parasol Switchback." This program comprised the modernization of Vietnamese troops and combat training of ethnic minority mountain tribes (*Montagnards*) by Special Forces so that they would be able to fight back against Communist attacks. Since campaigns directed against South Vietnam were starting to become more frequent in the neutral countries of Laos and Cambodia, the commander in chief assigned border-crossing operations to the Military Assistant Command Vietnam/Studies and Observation Group (MACV/SOG), an unconventional warfare unit that was established in 1964 and made up of personnel from the Army, the Navy, the Air Force and the Marines. For more than eight years, the SOG was used for jobs like sabotage, reconnaissance missions, psychological warfare and other secret operations throughout all of Southeast Asia. Out of necessity, much of the equipment furnished to the SOG by the CISO, such as clothing, arms, munitions and knives, was completely unmarked and was therefore not obviously of American origin. Jungle warfare was utterly dissimilar to the conventional warfare of the past. The CISO designed many objects such as backpacks, land mines, airborne supply containers, rations and body bags. My job

■ Conrad "Ben" Baker with the "SOG Bowie" and "SOG Recon" knives he designed.

was to come up with knives. After a few unsuccessful attempts, I eventually designed eight kinds of machetes and three kinds of tactical combat knives of undeterminable origin for SOG and Special Forces units. While the six-inch Bowie knife represented a combination of a tool and a weapon, the seven-inch "Recon" was a pure combat knife. I designed both this knife and the machetes with pointed blades that bent under in order to give the user more leverage. My third knife, called the "SCUBA/DEMO," had a seven-inch blade with a blunt saw to cut silk and was designed for deployment by the chief naval advisor of the SOG during appropriate naval special operations.

In 1970 I received a beautiful Böker switchblade from a friend of mine who worked for the CIA. During the next four years that I was in Asia I carried this knife in my backpack, but I never found out anything about its history. Thirty years later, the above-mentioned knife led me to the Böker Baumwerk and hence to Dietmar Pohl, head of the design and marketing department. For nearly two decades, Dietmar Pohl has been a passionate collector of combat and tactical knives. Countless of his tactical and utility knives are used by heads of special police forces and customs officers in Germany and are exported worldwide. The design of his "Speedlock" switchblade clearly demonstrates his versatility. His book *Tactical Knives* was written after years of painstaking research. It will prove relevant to those who use knives in their professions, historians and collectors alike.

To get to the heart of the matter: Major John Plaster described me in his book *SOG – A Photo History* as the American counterpart to James Bond's brilliant weapons expert "Q." However, I bow to Dietmar Pohl in recognition of his status as a truly gifted designer who picked up on the differences in our introductions to the field of tactical combat knives and has raised sharpened steel to new heights with his innovations, groundbreaking improvements in materials, and persistence.

Introduction

Tactical knife—the term was coined in the United States in the early 1990s. But what exactly are tactical knives, and who uses them? This question and others—from the evolution and design of these knives to the materials used to create them and the means of carrying them—will be answered for the first time in this comprehensive work. Not only are the various producers and their models introduced, but also in addition, the special forces for whom tactical knives are principally manufactured are described. Such topics as damascene swords, exotic handle materials, the care of knives, etc., will not be found in this book. For that, the reader is referred to general literature on knives.

Three influences have strongly inspired my personal viewpoint about tactical knives. First, the knives of manufacturer Jimmy Lile (died 1991) who, during the early 1980s, breathed new life into the field with his survival knives, thereby simultaneously laying laid the foundation for later developments in the area of tactical knives. Even then, his designs for combat knives foretold a time when other companies, which didn't even exist yet, would number among the established manufacturers of tactical knives.

Second, the ideas and designs of close-range combat expert Rex Applegate (died 1998), whose acquaintance I made at the 1996 SHOT show in Dallas. Although there existed an age difference of more than 50 years between us, we respected one another's ideas and expertise. When Applegate attended the 1997 International Weapons Exhibition (IWA) in Nürnberg,

■ **Rex Applegate and the author at the 1997 "SHOT Show" in Las Vegas.**

I was responsible for looking after him for nine days. During that time he told me many war stories—and not just once! Applegate's philosophy about tactical knives was rather one-sided and strongly influenced by the British WWII Fairbairn-Sykes Commando dagger. He saw the knife purely as a close-range combat weapon with which one sneaked up silently on an enemy from behind in order to kill him. The knife-fight experiences of close-range combat instructor William Ewart Fairbairn, which he gathered as a police officer in 1930's Shanghai, influenced Applegate during his own lifetime. If a knife's blade did not have two cutting edges, it was not a combat knife. For Rex Applegate, knives with a single cutting-edged blade remained pure field knives.

Even more than Lile's survival knives and Applegate's scintillating stories of classic night-time commando operations with dagger drawn, the experiences and insights of special police units with regard to their use of knives as tools influenced my view of tactical knives. Not until I engaged in friendly discussions and communal projects with them had the true needs of professional users of knives been brought to my attention. Thus, according to my personal point of view, the tactical knife is ultimately a conjunction of tool and weapon.

To give the reader the most well-rounded picture of tactical knives possible, this work also touches on combat knife developments from the WWI and WWII periods up to the Vietnam War. The main point, however, is how they contrast with the modern designs of the last two decades.

I would like to thank everyone who made this book possible through their support, particularly the special forces who expressed their confidence in me. In this regard I owe thanks to Hanspeter Kittel, Martin Hartmann and Jürgen Sohnemann for their considerable involvement. I would probably never have been able to gain insight into the world of police and military special forces without the help of my friends Bernd Soens, Michael Remig and Rüdiger Gaza. I would like to thank all three of them herewith for their support and their confidence in me. In terms of photography, Thomas Ruhl offered me his support; he sacrificed so much of his time for this project.

I thank the firms of Heinr. Böker Baumwerk, Heckler & Koch, Schwiedergoll – Die Klinge, Messerschmiede Nohl, Messermanufaktur Klötzli, HBS Marketing, Odins Klinge, ACMA Reus, Mediguard, Peter Hoffmann Import, Def-Tech, Nowar and C. Jul. Herbertz for the numerous photo samples of their products which they made available.

Likewise, heartfelt thanks go out to Tobias Leckebusch, who not only willingly let me have his collection of photographs, but also went out of his way to lend support for this project.

Proof of unparalleled trust was shown me by Conrad "Ben" Baker, who put at my disposal never-before published, personal photographs and partially confidential

information about the MACV/SOG in Vietnam. Despite his health limitations, time and again he took the time to answer probing questions in a completely selfless manner and to search his archive for rarities.

I also owe great thanks to my colleagues at the firms of Heinr. Böker Baumwerk and Boker USA, Inc., who each have contributed in his or her own way to the success of this book.

Finally, I would like to thank Martin Benz, Gray Randall, Frank Sigman, Wally Hayes, Anne Reeve and Jim Wagner for their invaluable support.

Solingen, July 2001

Dietmar Pohl

■ The author takes advantage of an opportunity to talk shop about tactical knives during a public demonstration of the GSG 9.

What Characterizes a Tactical Knife?

The term "tactics" denotes "a clever, strategic plan to achieve a certain goal." The goal behind the tactical knife is to reveal the greatest possible number of uses of a single instrument. This means the knife must serve equally as a weapon and as a tool—just the opposite of a double-edged combat dagger, which is designed purely to kill and maim. Of course, the tactical knife should also accomplish these tasks in offensive or defensive situations, but the reality is that most knives utilized by professionals such as soldiers and police officers are used mainly for so-called non-lethal tasks, whether for cutting ropes and belts in precarious situations or jimmying open a window. In the past, only a few knives have been developed with the basic idea of fulfilling both purposes. This becomes especially clear with the example

■ Tactical knives—equal parts tools and weapons. These models from German knife manufacturers Daniel Renner, Stefan Steigerwald, Peter Herbst and Bernhard Zwicker (left to right) are proof that such handmade knives are also successfully produced throughout the world.

of the British Fairbairn-Sykes Commando dagger, which was developed during WWII. The sole function of this sharpened stiletto-shaped knife was the destruction of vital human organs. However, its simultaneous usefulness as a tool was largely ruled out. The result was that soldiers carried at least two knives with them during military operations. It was just as much the doubled weight as the fact that in certain situations a knife had to be used immediately and for totally different purposes that explained the tactical need for just *one* multipurpose knife. Today it is not difficult to find this type of knife on the market. Nearly every manufacturer produces at least one model or even a whole assortment of knives that have tactical utility value. Based on the large supply and the continuing development of styles, materials and production engineering, it becomes hard to stick to a general overview. Therefore, the models discussed in this book can only be considered current up to a certain point in time.

■ **Two WWI German trench daggers and an Austrian trench knife (left).**

Combat Knives of WWI and WWII

Whoever wants to get the most complete picture of the development of knives in the 20th century and their use in modern warfare must not neglect WWI and WWII combat knives. In 1914, German troops in the west advanced quickly through Belgium and northern France. However, just before the end of the first year of the war, the front lines were paralyzed in positional warfare. On both sides there were no longer any decisive successes and an extensive network of trenches soon stretched over the battleground. Attempts to turn the situation around through massive advances generally failed and mostly led to a high death toll. For such assaults it was very important to gather as much information as possible about the strength of the enemy's troops and reinforcements. This was the responsibility of reconnaissance and raiding parties, who already were conceptually distinct from patrol missions that had been traditionally used up to that point in time. Often these mostly nighttime operations ended up being suicide missions, because many wounded soldiers and prisoners would be brought along on the arduous retreat and the enemy, having been alerted, would open fire from behind. Because less-cumbersome handguns were usually carried during such missions, the bayonet, which was created for infantry attacks, proved wholly inappropriate. Both sides began zealously to create improvised trench knives. Bayonet blades were shortened to a convenient size and sharpened, or a piece of metal post from a barbed-wire fence was simply reworked until it formed a handle and blade (the so-called "French nail").

When the German troops made their pressing need for trench knives known, a large number of steel works manufacturers began to come up with different designs. The vast majority of these knives more or less resembled one another, with a single- or double-edged blade approximately 15 centimeters long fitting flush over a hand guard, an angled grooved wooden handle, and a black sheet-steel sheath. One of the most striking trench knives was the DEMAG dagger made by the Deutschen Maschinenfabrik AG in Duisburg. Because of its bent metal handle, it was even capable of being fixed to a rifle or carbine 98. Besides officially issued service weapons, there was also a whole gamut of privately made trench knives and combat knives at the front. When the Americans entered the war in 1917, they outfitted their troops on the western front with a special close-range combat tool: they united two weapons, combining a thrusting blade with a knuckleduster. This "knuckle knife" drastically changed the way knives were used: their utility as tools was largely eliminated and the focus of the battle shifted primarily to combat and attack. These and other knife developments during WWI quite clearly demonstrate how "pure" weapons suited the altered tactical conditions of trench warfare.

During WWII not much had changed on the German side with regard to the concept of combat knives. By and large the Germans reverted to tried and true styles and merely changed the metal sheaths. Metal clasps replaced the leather belt loops,

■ **A weapon made purely for stabbing and beating: knuckle knife of American origin with three-sided blade.**

Photo: Deutsches Klingenmuseum Solingen/Lutz Hoffmeister

■ The most well known combat knives from the German side (from top): two examples of the "Infanteriemesser 42," the "Luftwaffenmesser" and the "Puma-Nahkampfmesser" with characteristic red Bakelite handle. A hallmark of WWII German close-range combat knives is the clamping devices on the sheath whereby they can be easily attached to the field shirt, in the boot shaft or on other clothing parts. Note the distinctive carrying mechanism. The usual belt loop would have limited the method of carrying the knife to on the belt. In this respect these sheath clips are indirectly among the forerunners of modern knife carrying systems.

Photo: Martin Benz/Karl Kost collectionCollection

and this enabled knives to be attached not only to the belt, but also to other parts of the uniform or equipment. Credit can therefore be given to the designers and manufacturers of these knives for having created the first tactical carrying possibilities.

Puma's close-range combat knife, with its characteristic red Bakelite handle, is among the best-known representatives of this type. New with this model was the use of shockproof synthetic material for the handle (see page 130). (*Verify upon layout.) As well as being suitable as a weapon, the sharpened, slightly curved single-edged blade was excellently suited for use as a field and utility knife. In 1942 the *Wehrmacht* introduced the "Infanteriemesser 42." Molded in a die, this sleek, efficient knife lacked a separately mounted handle. For the handle covering the manufacturer reverted again to wood. The *Luftwaffe* also issued to members of its air force field division and paratroopers (who at that time belonged to the air force) the so-called "Luftwaffen-Kampfmesser," which likewise resembled WWI trench knives in its construction and had a sharpened double-edged blade. On the other hand, the most technically interesting German knife—albeit not the most suitable for battle—was the "Fliegerkappmesser," which was introduced on May 24, 1937, and was issued to flight personnel as well as to paratroopers. In contrast to later close-range combat knives, its utility as a tool comes to the fore. Originally, the idea and intent behind its development was to outfit airplane crews with a compact knife that would allow its owner to use it with one hand in the cramped cockpit or fuselage of an airplane, and most importantly, when hanging from a parachute.

■ **For air force personnel and paratroopers: the 1937 "Fliegerkappmesser M." The unlockable pin was helpful when loosening knots and performing other tasks, but it was probably also used in close-range combat from time to time.**

This particularly proved to be advantageous if a parachute got caught in a tree or other impediment: the parachutist could secure himself with one hand and quickly cut himself free from the lines and belt apparatus. Moreover, he merely had to release the levered locking device and the blade would slip out because of its own weight and lock up. The British were so clearly impressed by this knife that they immediately had the firm of George Ibberson & Co. construct one in a slightly altered style.

On the Allied side, an entire range of new developments found its way to the troops. Probably the best-known knife is the "Fairbairn-Sykes Commando" dagger. The genesis of the Commando goes back to an idea of Lieutenant Colonel Dudley Clarke, who, shortly after the humiliating defeat of the English at Dunkirk, was able to convince the British government to establish a special forces unit that would carry out surprise attacks on selected targets with a minimum of support and relying on themselves alone. Among those who trained these special forces were former police officers William

■ Third model of the "Fairbairn-Sykes Commando" dagger, today produced by Wilkinson Sword.

Photo: Böker Baumwerk

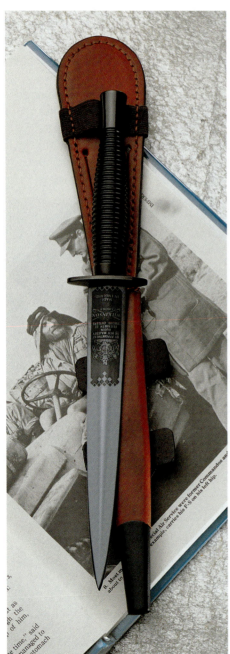

Ewart Fairbairn and Eric Anthony Sykes, who were able to gain experience in street and hand-to-hand combat in the teeming South Chinese harbor city of Shanghai, which at the time still belonged to the British Empire. The philosophy which that they shared with members of the Commandos was simply: "Kill or get killed!" Yet the first knives that the new commando troops received were anything but useful for their missions. The "BC 41" was a knuckle knife designed after the type used in WWI, and the "RBD" was nothing more than a simple hunting knife.

In November 1940, Fairbairn and Sykes established a relationship with the Wilkinson Company. Together they were able to interest the company's head, John Wilkinson-Latham, in creating a new kind of combat knife. By January 1941 Wilknoson began production of the "Fairbairn-Sykes Dagger" ("F-S" for short), named after both of its creators. During the course of the war the knife was also produced by other manufacturers in various models. The "F-S" dagger also served as a model for the American special forces. The dagger that was used for the American secret service branch, the Office for Strategic Services (OSS), as well as the "Marine Raider Stiletto," designed by Lieutenant Colonel Shuey, cannot hide their origins. Shuey had gone through training of the British commandos in Scotland, and this obviously served as his inspiration. Another of Fairbairn's favorite knives was the so-called "Smatchet." A massive chopping knife with a broad, leaf-shaped blade, it could be used as a weapon as well as a tool. A counterpart was likewise introduced by the OSS. One knife that became world-famous under the name "KA-BAR" and remains in use today by armies around the globe is the "U.S. Navy & Marine Corps Utility Knife Mk II." Officially introduced by the Marines in late 1942, the blade is strongly informed by the traditional Bowie shape and shows as a typical characteristic of American combat knives a grip composed of glued and pressed leather rings. The "Mk II" could be used as a weapon as well as a tool and fulfills even today, in the modified "Next Generation" model, the requirements of a modern tactical knife. With the "Trench Knife M 3" model, the U.S. Army obtained its own combat knife. In contrast to the Bowie blade of the "Mk II," the designers of the "M 3" chose a symmetrical blade in the shape of a spear point, which, again, was intended for close-range

■ **Right: German Waffen-SS soldiers during the 1944 Ardennes offensive. Indispensable in close-range combat: combat knives and shovels. The gunner on the left carries his knife—thanks to the sheath clip—"tactically" on the neck opening of his field shirt.**

Photo: Imperial War Museum/EA48004

combat. The upper portion of the handle was bent forward so that the thumb could be supported when thrusting.

The First Special Service Force, composed of American and Canadian soldiers, was equipped with a totally different knife. The design of the "V-42" model, produced by Case Cutlery, was a stiletto-shaped dagger blade with a thumb support. Exactly 3400 of the "V-42"s were produced by Case CutleryCase Cutlery produced exactly 3,400 of the "V-42s". Another Case Cutlery model is the "V-44 Survival Machete."

■ Still produced today: U.S. Army "Camillus M-3" and Marines "KA-BAR Mk-II."

Employed above all as a component of survival equipment for pilots, many of these Bowie knives went to the Marines fighting in the Pacific theater. Even in faraway Australia, combat knives began to be built: both the Australians and the U.S. troops stationed in that country obtained the "Australian Commando Knife" with its strongly hook-shaped pommel, which various manufacturers from "down under" produced.

Besides these officially issued knives, American GIs, of course, also carried a number of privately acquired knives. The most popular were models by John Ek, Murphy Knives, and Randall Made Knives. The John Ek knives are very simply made, but are characterized by their tremendous stability. No wonder: in contrast to the "F-S" dagger, Ek made the handle out of a single piece and designed the blade with a massive middle section. On the other hand, the "Murphy Combat" knife, made by the David Murphy Company of Portland, Oregon, was strongly reminiscent of an ordinary kitchen knife. The aluminum-coated handle made it extremely stable as well as resistant to the elements. The company made around 90,000 knives during the war. The knives made by Randall Made Knives of Orlando, Florida, were essentially more exclusive. The design of the Model 1 "All-Purpose Fighting Knife" was drawn up in 1942 by William "Bo" Randall together with young Lieutenant James Zacharias, who at the time was stationed in Orlando and wanted an "infallible" knife for his impending tour of duty overseas. Among the famous customers who carried Randall combat knives during WWII were future U.S. presidents John F. Kennedy and Ronald Reagan, as well as the previously mentioned hand-to-hand combat specialist Rex Applegate, author of an instruction manual for combat knives.

Both world wars brought a whole series of new discoveries with regard to the development of combat knives, for example, the optimal size for hand-to-hand combat or the importance of a matte finish for the blade during nighttime operations. These considerations continue to be found in modern tactical knives.

■ Developed for American Special Service forces (from top): "OSS Smatchet," "1st Special Service Force V-42 Stiletto" (both from Case Cutlery) and "Marine Raider Stiletto" from Camillus.

Photo: Thomas Ruhl

A combat knife highly sought after then as now: Randall Model 1 "All-Purpose Fighting Knife."

During the Korean War, on the other hand, there were no noteworthy new developments; for the most part, knives that were still stored in the arsenals from WWII were used. Most American and British combat knives are still produced by the original manufacturers or by other firms under license. German combat knives on the other hand are found only as contemporary originals, if one does not consider a few copies made by the meanwhile defunct Solingen company Anton Wingen ("Othello").

Influences and Developments During the Vietnam War

In the early 1960s, when the United States became involved in Indochina in an attempt to thwart Communist influence in Southeast Asia after the withdrawal of the French, probably no one guessed the war would last well into the 1970s. Among the first American soldiers whom the U.S. government sent into the area were so-called military advisors. These were members of the Special Forces, an elite unit that was strongly supported by President John F. Kennedy and that was devoted to unconventional warfare. Before long, however, the U.S. had sunk deeper and deeper into the whirlpool of the war. By the 1960s, the war, which up until then had been covert, had already become increasingly more open, and more and more U.S. troops were coming to Vietnam. The Special Forces, in particular, were in great need of special equipment including, of course, combat knives and machetes. If these essential items were not included among the officially supplied equipment, they were immediately created on the private market right away.

One of the most popular privately manufactured knives in the Special Forces was Gerber's "Mark II," designed by Army Captain C. A. "Bud" Holzmann in 1966. After a relatively short development phase, the first knives were sent to Vietnam as early as 1967. The aluminum handle of the "Mark II" was sprayed with molten high-grade steel in order to increase its non-slip quality, which was called "cat tongue" in technical jargon. Gerber bent the sides of the handle forward so that the user's thumb would be better supported after effecting a thrust. Various opinions exist as to the purpose of the inward-running radii of the "wasp-shaped" dagger blade. While some claim that the blade's shape made it easier to stick it through the ribs, others believe that it was merely an ergonomic design that made it easier to pull the knife from its sheath. The former head of the company, Pete Gerber, informed the author that he could reliably confirm only the latter assertion. However, since Holzmann is regarded as an idiosyncratic character, Gerber does not entirely rule out the first possibility. During the Vietnam War the knife was produced with a gray handle, black hilt and pommel and brown leather sheath.

American soldiers in Vietnam used not only the Gerber "Mark II," but also models by John Ek and handmade knives by Randall Made Knives and Gil Hibben. Included on the official supply lists were the "KA-BAR," whose value had already been proven in the course of two wars, and the "M 1963" survival knife, which had been introduced by the Air Force. The latter was similar to a "KA-BAR" in that the knife had a burnished Bowie blade and a leather handle. In addition, the knife had a serrated back edge and included a whetstone that fit into a front pocket on the

■ **One of the main tasks of the Special Forces in Vietnam: training Montagnards (members of mountain tribes unrelated to the Vietnamese) as fighters in the Civilian Irregular Defense Group (CIDG). In the background: the first head of the CISO, Captain David Watts.**
Photo: Conrad Baker

sheath. In order to prevent the knife from being a hindrance on the pilot's survival vest, its total length was reduced to 25 cm. The original manufacturer, Marbles Gladstone, produced the highest quality version of the knife, but soon orders were also given to other companies such as Camillus or Othello, who were able to offer cheaper versions of the same model. In doing so, unfortunately, craftsmanship was also compromised. The tip and back of the sheath also contained a metal plate for the wearer's protection.

The knives of the Military Assistant Command Vietnam/Studies and Observation Group (MACV/SOG for short) were likewise officially issued. For many years there circulated only incomplete or false information about the history of this legendary knife's development. In part because of the internationally disputed operations of American Special Forces in countries like Cambodia and Laos, the knife's origins are untraceable. The Studies and Observation Group functioned only as a cover in order to conceal the real objectives of the Special Forces. The term Special Operations Group, as they were sometimes called, more clearly delineated their actual responsibilities.

Established in January 1954, the MACV/SOG consisted of members of all four branches of the military, including Navy SEALs, the Marine Force Recon, specially trained Air Force pilots of the 90th Special Operation Wing and Army Special Forces,

■ Left: After successful completion of training: CIDG soldiers of the Mobile Strike Force together with a specialist of the 5th Special Forces Group.
Photo: Conrad Baker

■ Developed into the most popular privately manufactured knife of the Special Forces in Vietnam: the "Gerber "Mark II." Here, the original model from the 1960s.
Photo: Thomas Ruhl

The 1963 "U.S. Air Force Survival Knife M" from Camillus, officially issued to the troops.

also known as Green Berets, who comprised the majority of the group. The Marines in particular participated in secret missions in North Vietnam. The Navy SEALs knew their way around the port of Haiphong especially well as the result of espionage. The MACV/SOG carried out secret operations throughout Southeast Asia in close cooperation with the American intelligence service, the CIA (Central Intelligence Agency). Among other things, they worked in close cooperation with the Vietnamese Special Exploitation Service (SES). Their goal was to uncover possible acts of sabotage, intelligence procurement and other secret missions. At its peak, the MACV/SOG comprised of approximately 2,000 Americans and more than 8,000 Vietnamese. Their duties included the following:

1. Border-crossing operations into Cambodia, Laos and North Vietnam to obtain intelligence and carry out commando missions.

2. Gathering information about prisoners of war and possible rescue missions.

3. Rescuing air crews shot down in enemy territory (so-called "Bright Light" missions).

4. Training, smuggling and supervising agents in North Vietnam and establishing a resistance movement.

5. Combating psychological warfare waged by the enemy as well as operating a secret radio station in North Vietnam.

6. Abducting or eliminating high-ranking enemy operatives.

7. Recreating missing secret documents and apparatus created by the enemy.

8. Smuggling defective hand grenades and other faulty munitions into enemy arsenals.

MACV/SOG operations officially ended in 1973, but obviously there were still some American Special Forces who were active in Southeast Asia until after the fall of Saigon in 1975.

■ **Hibben handmade more than 300 knives of the "Jungle Fighter" model for members of U.S. Special Forces in Vietnam.**

■ Briefing of a MACV/SOG recon team. The platoon leader (right) has secured his KA-BAR knife to his belt in classic Vietnam fashion.

Photo: Conrad Baker

Conrad "Ben" Baker and the Secret Knives of the MACV/SOG

The history of these knives is entangled in great secrecy. This is very easy to understand because, even today, many of the operations in which they were employed are classified "top secret." The man responsible for the design of these knives unwillingly became an extremely successful knife designer.

In June 1963 Conrad Baker ("Ben" to his friends), acting head of the newly created Counter-Insurgency Support Office ("CISO" for short), was stationed in Okinawa. Among the CISO's top-secret duties was the logistical support of paramilitary training camps in Southeast Asia under the direction of Special Forces. In addition, it was responsible for a limited research and development program for Special Forces. The CISO received its instructions directly from the CIA. When the MACV/SOG carried out its first secret missions in Vietnam and Laos in 1964, the CISO was responsible for its support within that territory. There quickly emerged an increasing need for equipment whose origins did not give its owners away and which was therefore completely "sterile." Knives and machetes were among the first things that were

desperately needed in the jungle. The CIA immediately produced knives of European and Asian make. However, none of the members of the Special Forces seemed truly happy with this solution. Of course, each member of the Special Forces had his own concept of the ideal design for a knife. However, the suggestions that were submitted yielded nothing close to a uniform picture of what the urgently needed military knives should look like. Baker was thus assigned the task of designing the most practical cutting tool possible that the majority of the Special Forces would like.

Baker chose a 1920s hunting knife from Marbles Gladstone as the model for the handle. According to his estimation, the handle, which was made out of pressed and glued leather rings, was ideal for the future SOG knife. Baker invested countless hours of work developing the handle so that it would hold up in life-threatening combat situations and under the worst conditions imaginable. Prototypes of the knife bearing the mark "SOG Recon" were put to the test in Okinawa under conditions that were as realistic as possible. From the beginning, the handle exhibited its final shape, with an oval profile and flat finger moldings so that the index finger could exercise maximum control over the blade from directly behind the lower part of the hilt. As for the hilt itself, Baker kept the traditional shape, stamped on both sides,

which in his view afforded full protection for the hand. The hilt was made of the same material as the pommel: molten brass, steel and aluminum. The aluminum version was provided to the troops through the official channels from the units, but was in part privately created. Various manufacturers made the "SOG Recon knife" with sharp handle points, although strictly speaking they were supposed to be round. To improve hand position and the center of gravity, however, these points could be easily shortened. According to Baker, he could scarcely refuse to accept a shipment just because the handle points were not round. After all, this was war! Besides providing optimal protection to the hand, the handle was supposed to lend support during twisting or pulling the blade out of a body or object. Along with the flat surface on the upper and lower side of the blade, the soldier could quite simply place his index finger around the blade thereby obtaining further support. In order to test this concept, Baker visited a local slaughterhouse and there performed

■ Insignia of the U.S. Special Forces and the Military Assistance Command Vietnam/Studies and Observation Group (MACV/SOG).

numerous stabbing tests on (dead) pigs. If the blade stuck deep in the chest or spine, it was generally very difficult to extract it. However, thanks to the new design of the blade and handle, this was no longer a problem. Of course, Baker came up with these considerations in the first place because the blade had to pierce through the uniform jackets and equipment of the enemy. The finger moldings stopped the hand from slipping if the handle was bloody or covered in

■ **Left: Conrad Baker in 1967 in front of CISO headquarters with his inventions for the MACV/SOG. In the foreground, the famous "Banana" machete.**
Photo: Conrad Baker

■ **Below: "SOG Recon" knife; top, the Hicks copy, bottom, the Vietnam original with Baker's drawing.**
Photo: Conrad Baker

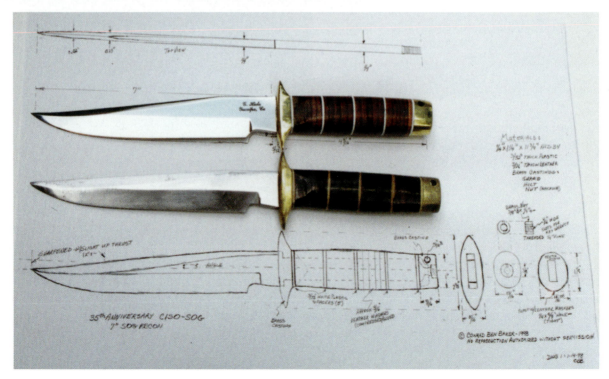

sweat. The knifemaker gave special attention to a sturdy, heavy handle for reasons of balance and stability. Baker, who never fancied himself as a knife designer, still wanted to make sure that the soldier could rely on his knife under the most extreme conditions.

He chose the blade from a wide range of forms, which were cut out of a 1/4-inch (ca. 6.4 mm) thick steel plate. These were quickly attached to a two halves of a handle that were made from a broomstick and duct taped together. These improvised knives were then tested for hand position, balance, and depth of thrust. According to Baker, Master Sergeant Ross Bailey, who was responsible for conducting the tests, still has not forgiven him for the blisters he got on his hand from trying to cut and stab trees with the unwieldy prototypes.

Baker preferred a hollow-back cutting edge to a solid-back cutting edge, even though the latter could be pulled out of a body more easily. The upward-curving knife point—in relation to the handle's axis —allowed for a deep thrust with a minimum of effort. The seven-inch blade (ca. 17.8 cm) was chosen as a pure combat blade; it stuck deeper but caused less trauma. The six-inch Bowie blade (ca. 15.2 cm) did not stick as deeply but caused more trauma, as the tests on the pigs clearly showed. The seven-inch "Recon" was issued exclusively to SOG reconnaissance scouts. Because of the numerous hand-to-hand combats in which SOG recon-naissance specialists were involved behind enemy lines, they placed great value on the longer blade. Some of the weapons that are found in military knife collections have a purple blade instead of a black one. This coloration was in no way intentional. It was caused by a particular blackening process that, unfortunately, simultaneously ruined the blade.

The sheaths were made out of brown, and later black, leather. The handle was so ingenious that it could be extracted with one hand, and the wearer would not be injured while pulling the knife out. On the front side of the sheath, a small pouch was sewn on and riveted which held a whetstone with two different grain sizes. Thus, giving the design and sample knives

■ Quang-Nam province in 1969, shortly before the military action: Member of the MACV/SOG with Colt CAR-15 assault rifle and "SOG Recon" knife on belt carrying device.

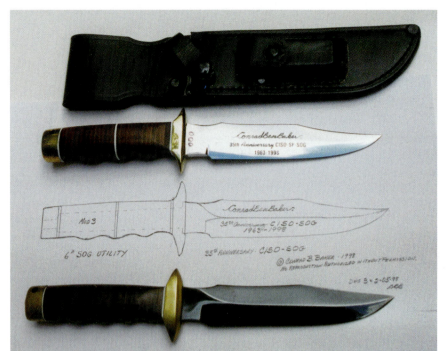

to the SOG/5th Special Forces was successful.

On June 6, 1964, Baker gave the design drawings to various Japanese knife manufacturers so they could create the prototypes. The CISO had to withdraw their first commission from the manufacturer, Japan Sword, because the steel quality was inferior. The choice of steel alloy settled on SKS-3, a chrome-molybdenum steel that has a hardness on the Rockwell scale of 55 to 57. Yogi Shokai eventually obtained the commission of more than 1,300 seven-inch "Recon" knives with blackened blades, including sheaths and whetstones, at a price of $9.85 each. A total of 1,308 knives were produced in Japan, including eight prototypes with polished blades. In October 1966 the company received a second commission for more than 1,200 six-inch Bowies with black sheaths for a unit price of $8.40. Many of these pieces were later chrome-plated as commemorative knives and decorated with engravings. One of these special models is the particular pride of Ben Baker.

In March 1967 an additional order was placed. This time, however, the knives were to be more properly accounted for and serially numbered

from 1 to 4,700. Using the typical military supply description "Knife, national production, hunting, six inches, black sheath with whetstone," each knife was given an exclusive serial number to identify it, which was etched into the right side of the blade. The term "national production" was chosen in order to pacify local politicians. The final production occurred in November 1967, and Baker is certain that all the knives were produced by the same manufacturer.

In 1967, the 5th Special Forces asked the CISO to help them purchase 1,700 commemorative knives of the six-inch Bowie variety. The back side the blade was to be engraved with the Special Forces insignia and the words "5th Special Forces Group (Abn)—Vietnam." The CISO promised their support, and Baker designed a model with a slightly altered blade back. In January 1968 the knives were issued and the Special Forces paid the bill.

Perhaps the CISO's most unusual knife was given to the SOG Naval Advisory Detachment ("NAD" for short) in Da Nang. The double-edged blade with a serrated back edge had a single-piece handle with a thickness of 1/4 inch (ca. 6.4 mm). For the blade material, one of the best rustproof alloys available at the time was chosen. Each of the 39 knives, which contained no identifying marks at all, was issued together with a brown sheath, a whetstone and a round file. In mid-1964, one knife was given to the CISO and the other 38 were issued to the NAD with the supply description "Knife, national production, SCUBA/DEMO, 7 1/4 inches." Thirty-six of these knives were later written off as a total loss during combat. Baker commented on this to the author: "Ask around in Hanoi what happened to the knives. They ought to know!"

An additional 50 knives of the six-inch Bowie variety were given to the Joint Casualty Resolution Center in Thailand in 1972. Whoever compares the various CISO knives can easily tell that they came from different workshops. This is because of the small differences in polishing, handle variations, etc. But these insignificant production variations were not grounds enough to justify another installment. The exceptions were those knives that were made of inferior steel. Even though the CISO did not order any metallurgical tests, it did insist on testing the flexibility and

■ **SCUBA/DEMO prototype for the SOG Naval Advisory Detachment. Only 39 of these knives were produced.**
Photo: Conrad Baker

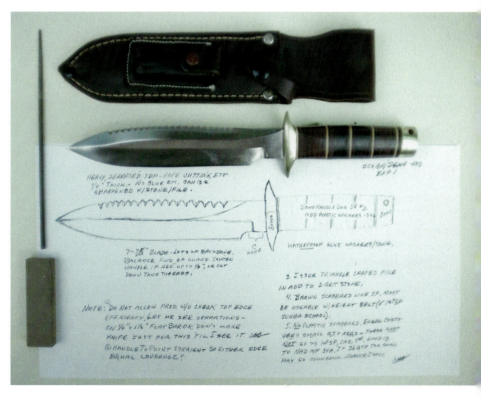

■ **Also from Baker's drawing board: machetes for the MACV/SOG. Below, two designs of the "Banana" model.**
Photo: Conrad Baker

hardness of the blades. In this way they fully lost quality control from the Japanese manufacturers, as well as the reenlistment of those soldiers who had to use those knives in the jungle.

In addition to the knives mentioned above, Conrad "Ben" Baker also designed an entire series of machetes, the most famous of which was the "Banana."

Even though Baker became a knife designer unwillingly, today many knifemakers

and manufacturers still like to copy his six-inch Bowie blade. SOG Specialty Knives based itself on this model, so to speak, in the mid-1980s. Other companies like Al Mar, John Ek and Hattori were also drawn to Baker's design. In 1998, Baker gave knifemaker Gary Hicks permission to make a licensed reproduction of his handmade series. Hicks produced the seven-inch as well as the six-inch models. The first 100 pieces were available as a set with the same serial numbers, wall holders and certificates. Numbers higher than 100 could also be purchased individually. Beck's Cutlery from North Carolina became the exclusive distributor. After the appearance of this series, SOG Specialty Knives paid more attention to the seven-inch "Recon," as well as the less well-known SCUBA/DEMO model, which they still produce. Thus, Baker was never credited as the designer.

Although Ben Baker's models were designed primarily as combat knives in the 1960s, they are also consistent with tactical knives, according to the modern view-point.

Randall Made Knives in Vietnam

Some of the most sought-after knives of the Vietnam War are those made by Randall Made Knives. In the early 1960s the war—still secret—barely registered in the company's orders. The number of orders rose almost imperceptibly; most of the requests were for the classic WWII model Model 1 "All-Purpose Fighting Knife," the model Model 2 "Fighting Stiletto," and model Model 14 "Attack" and model Model 15 "Airman," which had been designed for the Marine Corps but was rejected, to the great disappointment of the company's president, William Randall.

■ A member of the Special Forces fashions an oil drum into a primitive shower using Baker machetes.

Photo: Conrad Baker

The interest in stainless steel blades was, however, obvious, and could be attributed to the humid climate of Southeast Asia. Also, synthetic materials like Tenite and, later, Micarta were preferred to leather for the handles. In mid-1965, when America entered the conflict in full force and thousands of U.S. soldiers were sent to Vietnam, a flurry of orders began. In order to become the market leader for these orders, Randall looked to the German city of Solingen to manufacture the pre-made blades for his models Models 14 and 15; these were die-cast and then ground into shape. The assembly and final polishing was then done in Orlando. Through this division of labor, the Americans were in a position to send the knives to the soldiers in Vietnam six weeks after they had been ordered. Usually the waiting time for a complete handmade Randall knife took up to one and a half years. In addition, because of this sensible new production process, prices dropped considerably. These knives could be recognized by the stamp on the blade reading "Randall Made Solingen."

■ **Gary and William "Bo" Randall assessing their Model 17 "Astro." This photograph was taken in the early 1960s.**

Photo: Randall Made Knives

However, with respect to Randall Made Knives, perhaps the most interesting development during the Vietnam War was the survival knife "Model 18."

In early January 1963, William Randall received a letter from Vietnam. The writer was Captain George W. Ingraham of the U.S. Army Medical Corps, who at that time was serving in the 94th Medical Detachment as and flew a CH-21C. He described very precisely to Randall what happened when a soldier in an airplane or helicopter had to make an emergency landing in the jungle. He had to immediately free himself from the cabin and then build a dugout, look for water, possibly engage in hand-to-hand combat with communist guerrillas and signal a rescue airplane. After careful study of the Randall catalog, he had

come to the conclusion that a Model 14 was the most suitable knife for the job, although it would have to be modified according to him. The following alterations should be made:

■ **Randall Model 15 "Airmen." A smaller model of this combat knife was developed for the Marines.**

1. The back of the knife should be serrated to render it suitable for cutting oneself free through the aluminum lining or Plexiglass cockpit of an airplane.

2. The pommel should be changed to the form of a D-ring, in order to allow it to be used in hand-to-hand combat to strike the enemy.

3. The handle should be in the form of a tube that would be waterproof when screwed together and would offer room for survival equipment. This equipment, according to Ingraham, would consist of matches, water purification tablets and medicine.

To Randall, Ingraham described why he wanted to see all of these properties in a single knife: An airplane evacuation took a matter of seconds, and nobody had the time to look for his survival equipment, emergency rations, weapons, etc. If the

machine was already burning and the fuel tank could explode at any moment, it was simply: "Get out!" At the same time, with the right tool one could also help a comrade who was trapped in the rear, in that one could smash through the cockpit, saw off the side of the aircraft or cut through his belt. With the new multipurpose knife on his belt, he could solve all these problems at once. In order to clarify his description of the ideal knife, Ingraham enclosed a drawing.

Randall mulled over the Captain's suggestions for over a week, and then wrote him with a heavy heart to say that while he understood the rationale for wanting such changes, it was technologically impossible for his factory to produce such a knife. The challenge was just too great. Together with his son Gary he discussed the possibilities, and just one and a half weeks later, three prototypes had been produced. Two were to be sent to Captain Ingraham to try out and one would remain at the factory as a model. Randall sent the knife to Vietnam and explained the following: The serrated edge had been successfully tested on a metal trash can. The screwed-together handle was impossible because they could not cut threads at their factory. So they were looking for an appropriate cap. After discovering that

■ **Special Forces member (far left) with Randall Model 15 "Airmen" on his belt.**

Photo: Randall Made Knives

■ **Captain Ingraham's original hand sketch, obtained in Vietnam by William Randall.**

Randall Made Knives Archive

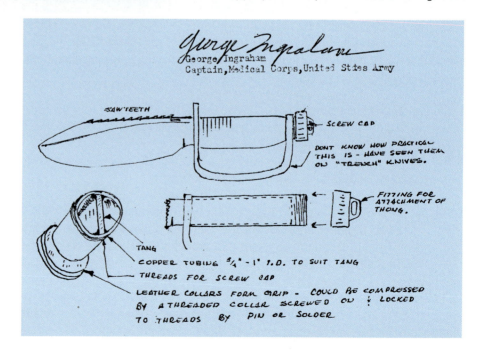

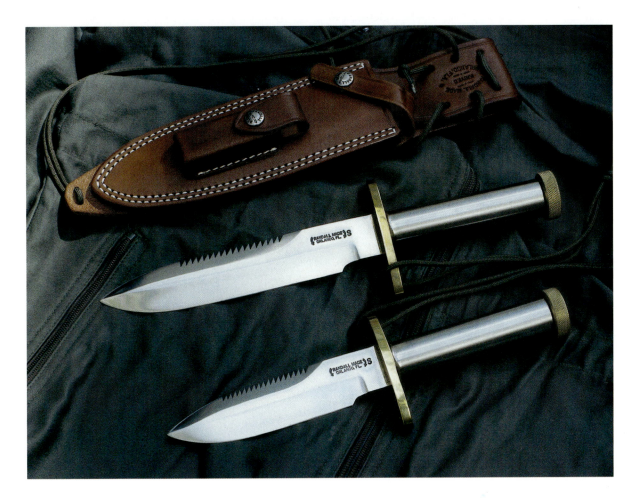

gearshifts were not available in the right sizes, Randall found an cap made out of synthetic material, which was actually meant to be the end of a lawn chair leg. In order to keep the cap from rusting, duct tape could be stuck to the metal handle. Furthermore, he suggested that the entire handle be wrapped in duct tape so that the handle, which was admittedly very smooth, did not slip out of the hand. The knife could be securely carried in the Model 14 and Model 15 C-sheaths which were already provided and which came with a whetstone.

Ingraham proved highly enthusiastic about the new knife. Just a short time later, Randall included it as a regular Model 18 "Attack/Survival" knife in his catalog. Other than Models 14 and 15, this design ended up being the most requested Randall knife in Vietnam. Years later, however, Randall was able to successfully offer a threaded closing mechanism made out of brass.

Randall's legendary Vietnam knives are still available today and are essentially unchanged. For tactical users, Randall produced Randall Models 1 and 2, which were also coated with Micarta and came with black leather sheaths.

■ **Randall Model 18 "Attack/Survival" with 7.5 and 5.5-inch blades, of modern construction, with brass breechblock cap.**

■ **Left: Marine infantry sergeant in Vietnam in 1968, with Randall Model 2.**

Photo: Randall Made Knives/Dan Dreger

New Trends in Knives in the Early 1980s

The 1970s were marked by the trauma of the Vietnam War. No American manufacturer dared to market any new developments in the field of combat knives. In Germany things were not much better. Only the field and paratrooper knives of the *Bundeswehr*, cheap copies of the KA-BAR, and bayonets were available on the market. In the 1980s this lull came to an abrupt end: Through the success of the movie *Rambo (First Blood)* and the survival knife used by its main character, made by Arkansas knife makerknifemaker Jimmy Lile, the knife industry gained new enthusiasm for the combat knife. Quite a few copies of this knife cropped up after 1983. Knife makers and manufacturers took part in this plagiarism. Even the tradition-rich firm Buck competed on the market with its "BuckMaster Survival" model which manufacturers from the Far East like to copy to this day. Yet, what was far more important was the fact that because of this initial enthusiasm, new developments with respect to survival knives occurred. Cold Steel made a buzz with its Tanto blade and dagger. In addition, the use of slip-resistant Elastomer

■ Left: Randall Model 1 as a tactical knife: modern model with Micarta handle and black leather sheath.

■ In the 1980s they created the image of the Vietnam fighter together with a survival knife: Jimmy Lile and Sylvester Stallone, with the "Rambo —The Mission" model in his hand.
Photo: Lile Handmade Knives

■ Below: A classic: Jimmy Lile's survival knife from the movie *Rambo (First Blood)*.

■ The most well-
known knives of the
1980s, from left:
"Buckmaster Survival"
(Buck), "Master Tanto"
(Cold Steel), "S.E.R.E."
(Al Mar), "TAC II"
(Gerber), "Bowie"
(SOG) and "Patriot"
(Gerber).

■ Early tactical clasp knives with so-called "lock back" clasps, from top: "S.E.R.E. Folder" (Al Mar), "Tomcat" (SOG) and "Winder I" (SOG).

elastomer as a handle material can clearly be attributed to Cold Steel. Gerber seized the opportunity and presented a great number of innovations in terms of survival and combat knives. The models "LMF" and "BMF" were strongly inspired by the Rambo trend. Gerber was also one of the first industrial manufacturers to use sand on its metal surfaces. Another handle innovation was the use of the soft material Hypalon, which allowed one to use the knife for chopping without fatigue. Gerber is also responsible for the wide distribution of Cordura sheaths, even though the company was not as lucky with its earlier camouflage versions. With its "Clipit" models, Spyderco was definitely among the vanguard of the one-handed folding knives with trouser clips. In the mid-1980s, SOG Specialty Knives came on the scene, copied Ben Baker's SOG Bowie—without his permission —thereby ensuring their success in the knife market (see page 28). Soon, a great number of SOG blade models appeared, as well as folding knives. At that time folding knives were generally equipped with blade locks in the back of the handle, so-called "Lock Back" closures.

The knife designer Al Mar also took the opportunity to present new kinds of combat knives. Its "S.E.R.E." designs for the Special Forces left a lasting impression on the knife market of the 1980s. The Solingen companies Schlieper and Anton Wingen tried to compete with these marvelous developments and produced survival and boot knives. However, unlike the American companies, they are no longer in existence today. Even the American manufacturer Kershaw with its "Trooper" model should not be ignored. In Spain, too, the new trends left their mark. The "Jungle King" survival knife by Aitor has almost achieved cult status. From Austria, Glock contributed its "Feldmesser" which, because of its modern design and its use of new synthetic materials quickly found a niche in the market; today it is part of the equipment of many armies around the globe.

Purchasing designs by famous knifemakers likewise found its roots in the 1980s.

Even if many knives from that decade are no longer available today, either because technology has advanced or because the demand simply no longer exists, they nevertheless belong to the forerunners of a new concept—the idea behind the tactical knives of the 1990s.

Developments by Close-Range Combat Specialist Rex Applegate

Among the most enigmatic personalities in the field of tactical knives is Colonel Rex Applegate. As a recognized close-range combat specialist he could, up until his death in 1998, transform his vast experience and numerous ideas into practical knives. In order to fully understand his contribution, his personality must first be examined more closely.

In 1939, after completing his studies in economics at the University of Oregon, Applegate enlisted in the U.S. Army. In March 1942, after serving three years in the military police, he was transferred to the (then still unknown) special department Coordinator of Information ("COI" for short), which later was renamed the Office for Strategic Services ("OSS" for short). Under the command of Colonel Bill Donovan, Applegate had to establish a secret training camp for agents in Thurmont, Maryland. In order to gain the necessary experience in the area of hand-to-hand combat, Applegate was to make the unusual acquaintance of convicted murderers and violent criminals, who gave him his first insights into stabbing and strangulation. Soon after that, he was sent to Great Britain, where he deepened his knowledge with the Commando forces and the Special Operation Executive ("SOE" for short). At the SOE training camp in Achnacarry, Scotland, he met for the first time Captain Eric Anthony Sykes, the co-designer of the "F-S Commando" dagger. Sykes, who was drawn more to pistols than to knives, familiarized Applegate with instinctive close-range shooting. A stronger influence on Applegate, however, was the hand-to-hand combat expert William Ewart Fairbairn, with whom he later was to develop two important knives. In late 1942, Fairbairn was transferred to the OSS, where he met Applegate for the first time. Under Fairbairn's leadership Applegate quickly developed into an expert in all facets of armed and unarmed hand-to-hand combat. As soon as 1943, he published the classic work on hand-to-hand combat techniques titled *Kill or Get Killed*, a book whichthat is still available today.

During their long shop talks, Applegate and Fairbairn dedicated themselves to developing combat knives. The combined experiences of the OSS agents and the British Commando soldiers built the foundation for their new developments. Fairbairn was pained to realize that the dagger he had developed with Sykes was seriously flawed. At 18 cm, the blade was much too long, and even though it was conically shaped it was still blunt and of no use in cutting. Even worse, the pointed blade broke off easily. Of course, this was also because of the poor quality of steel during the war.

Applegate remembered a Finnish mountain hunter who, after Stalin's attack on Finland during the Finno-Russian war in the winter of 1939-40, developed a special technique of killing Red Army soldiers. At night he would sneak up to the enemy on his skis and stab them to death lightning fast with his "Puuko." This all-purpose knife, typical of that country, is known for its razor sharpness and generally has a blade length of around 15 cm (although there obviously are shorter and longer ones as well). But 15 cm is long enough to pierce through thick winter clothing and reach vital organs. Based on this Finnish wisdom, Applegate and Fairbairn likewise set the blade length at 15 cm, at the same time strengthening the cutting edge and making the point rounder.

■ **He taught Applegate the rudiments of knife combat: William Ewart Fairbairn.**

Photo: Rex Applegate

The two practitioners also did not care for the spindle-shaped, narrow handle of the "F-S" dagger, which simply offered too little surface to grip. Besides, it was practically impossible for a user to figure out whether the cutting edge was horizontal or vertical, which could be a fatal situation during a night mission under high stress. The hand protection also left a lot to be desired. Correctly holding the knife in the fight stance pushed the thumb against the hand protector uncomfortably as soon as the blade met its target. In some cases this would even lead to the thumbnail being torn off. Consequently, Applegate and Fairbairn developed a completely new,

■ **From Applegate's collection: left, the "F-S Wilkinson Sword" dagger (a gift from Fairbairn); right, the "OSS" dagger from the Landers, Frary & Clark company.**

Photo: Böker Baumwerk/Bob Lum

ergonomic handle, which better took into account the anatomy of the hand.

In the OSS workshop some prototypes had already been constructed, but then the war ended, leaving the realization of this design unfinished. Applegate held on to the designs, but did not bring them out again until 1980 in order to submit them to knifemaker T. J. Yancey. Applegate and Yancey decided to realize the 40-year-old project at last.

The blade length of the new "A-F" knife was 15 cm and its point was broader than that of the "Fairbairn-Sykes" dagger. To increase its durability, the thickness of the blade was the same up until very close to the point. The thin and breakable round handle of the "Fairbairn-Sykes" was replaced by a sturdy flat handle infrastructure that ran almost the whole entire length of the handle. For the handle coating, the two chose Lexan, an extremely unbreakable polycarbonate synthetic material. The shape of the handle allowed for all grip possibilities and comfortably filled the hand. Notches in the area of the thumb and the index finger ensured that the knife lay correctly in the hand without the user having to look at it. Long grooves on the sides of the handle were meant to keep it from rolling around in the hand. An additional feature of the handle was a balancing lead weight that served as a counterweight to the blade. Now the user could weight his own knife according to personal preference. The ends of the brass hand protector were curved forward to take pressure off the thumb. A leather sheath, manufactured by the holster maker Tex Shoemaker, completed the tactical requirements of the knife.

■ **Two generations of handmade Applegate-Fairbairn knives: left, T. J. Yancey's knife; right, William Harsey's knife.**

Unfortunately, with a price tag of $350, the knife was far too expensive for the budget of the average soldier. In the quest for a cheaper version of his knife, Applegate turned to Al Mar Knives and Black Jack Knives. In the long run, however, neither American manufacturer suited him in terms of production and quality, so he canceled his contracts with both companies. Ultimately, the German firm Böker took over production. Applegate found in this Solingen company a manufacturer who could make his knife according to his specifications. Because the old tools to make the handle were no longer available, Böker made some changes to the knife. The most important changes in comparison to its forerunners were the partially dovetailed 440-C steel blade, two high-grade steel handle weights in place of the lead weights, and the Kydex sheath. Alternatively, one could choose a version with a flat blade and a Cordura sheath.

However, Applegate's thirst for action was not quenched with the making of this knife. Another knife that lay close to the retired Colonel's heart was the so-called "Smatchet," whose name is an amalgamation of the words "smash" and "machete." Again it was Fairbairn who taught Applegate the subtleties of this instrument. Incidentally, WWII British propaganda used the amazingly effective tactic of showing Commando soldiers in together with their "Smatchets" on posters and in photographs. Applegate and Fairbairn realized that the usefulness of the leaf-shaped blade was greatly increased by sharpening it on both sides. Once again prototypes were built, but in this case as well the war ended before the series could be completed.

■ **Teamwork: Harsey's and Valloton's hinged Applegate-Fairbairn knives.**

■ The complete series of handmade Applegate-Fairbairn knives. Far right: the Applegate-Fairbairn "Tactical" knife belonging to Harsey and the author, modeled after a reworked design.

In the late 1980s, the "Smatchet" was given new life. Rex Applegate had a small number of pieces made by Buck and planned to market them under the name Wells Creek. After 500 pieces had been completed, another manufacturer took on the task of making the "Smatchet," this time Al Mar, who had already produced a version of the "A-F" knife. Since the year 2000, Böker has manufactured the "Smatchet." The design of the Böker model is strongly reminiscent of the prototypes from the OSS workshop and the handmade individual pieces of Bill Harsey (see page 110).

In the early 1990s, Applegate invented a series of innovative versions of his "A-F" knives, including three bootknife versions, two of which Böker likewise manufactured, and one folding knife. Applegate commissioned Gerber to make the folding knives, and they achieved notable success with this model.

In January 2001, subsequent to Applegate's death, the latest development of the "A-F" knife came out. Bill Harsey and the author created together created the "A-F Tactical" model, with an approximately one-inch (2.54 cm) longer blade and a handle infrastructure that protruded from the end of the handle and was suitable for breaking windowpanes.

Even though Applegate intended his knives to be used strictly as weapons, they served as the basis for a number of tactical considerations, which obviously underlay the developments in the field of tactical knives.

■ **Rex Applegate at over 80 years of age, proudly displaying the Applegate-Fairbairn knife developed by him and Fairbairn and produced by Black Jack.**
Photo: Rex Applegate/Black Jack Knives

Knives in Tactical Deployment

The fundamental question is this: Who uses tactical knives and for which tasks are they utilized in particular? First and foremost are police and military special forces, who, because of their unusual responsibilities, have to rely on special equipment. This of course includes, besides highly powerful firearms, the oldest tools known to mankind: knives. Because special forces are very reticent as far as their equipment is concerned (for understandable reasons) it is often quite difficult to come by this kind of information.

An immediate need for tactical knives exists also in the field of personal protection. The personal security guard can either have a government job or be employed by a private security organization. As opposed to the personal security guard who is supplied by the state, the private employee is not hindered by official restrictions and can therefore supply his own knives and carrying systems according to his personal needs and desires. While soldiers or officers of special forces may often wear their

■ **Military special forces and special units are among those who have a direct need to use tactical knives: KSK soldiers prepare to storm a building.**
Photo: BMVg

knives openly, the personal security guard needs to use them as discreetly and inconspicuously as possible during undercover operations for tactical reasons, in order to take advantage of the element of surprise. How these knives look when concealed will be elaborated on in a later chapter, beginning on page 112.

Of course, tactical knives are not built exclusively for use by professionals. Most of them are sold to private individuals who like to carry such knives for everyday use, or just enjoy collecting specialty knives. No doubt this group makes up the lion's share of the knife industry. Only a small number of high-priced knives are sold to members of special forces, even though knife manufacturers like to

■ In the U.S., members of the police force train offensively and defensively using a knife as a weapon.

Photo: HSS International

use such claims as an advertising strategy. Most of the time a test model is requested by a special unit in order to compare it against other products on the market, but it may never be adopted into the official supply list—yet right away the claim is: "The official knife of…!" The clearest example of this is the U.S. Navy SEAL knife. Over the years, many American manufacturers have claimed to be the official knife supplier of this elite group. Thus, it is quite understandable that most of the special forces prefer to remain silent on the subject. Consequently, the procurement authority will add a clause into the sales contract forbidding the manufacturer to mark the equipment with the unit's insignia or to advertise the fact that the unit uses that product. Of course, this causes great frustration to the manufacturer, because sales of his product would increase enormously on the free market were he able to use this in his advertisements.

The examples that are introduced in this book are the officially sanctioned tactical knives used in missions by such special forces as the *Kommando Spezialkräfte* of the *Bundeswehr*, the *Grenzschutzgruppe 9*, the *Spezialeinsatzkommandos* of the police force ("SEK") and the *Zentralen Unterstützungsgruppe Zoll*. Not considered here are privately acquired knives that many specialists have at their disposal and whose use is allowed or at least tolerated by the authorities. During the course of my research it became apparent that among the special forces, the same level of tactical use prevailed. The knife is seen and used primarily as a tool. Worldwide, use of knives as weapons has dropped greatly because of the use of modern, highly precise firearms. Moreover, in the case of border patrols, police officers and customs agents, using knives as weapons is even prohibited by law. This stands completely opposed to the situation in other countries, e.g., the United

States, where members of police special forces are trained in defensive strategies using knives as weapons. In Germany, only members of the *Bundeswehr* have the option of using knives as weapons in the scope of their duties.

So as not to have to continually repeat the functions of knives that are used in the duties of the special forces, some general examples are given here.

Emergency escapes
Time and again, scenarios arise in which someone is trapped by a rope on the wall of a building, on a bridge, or outside a helicopter. Cutting through safety belts in automobiles or airplanes also belongs to this category. In certain emergency situations, special forces, whose duties also include airborne operations, need knives to cut through parachute lines.

Obstacle removal during precision shooting
Here the knife proves to be an indispensable tool with which one can remove branches that are located in the field of vision or firing range, or other hindrances like tarps or curtains.

Field use
Knives can be useful for preparing food, including opening tin cans as well as dressing trapped or wounded animals. Likewise, knives are also useful for building shelters.

Barrier penetration
Often special forces run into a barrier that had not been identified even during careful reconnaissance and which must be removed or surmounted. In such scenarios, knives are mainly used as tools (i.e., a crowbar or a hammer). True, they are not exactly made for such tasks, but a quality product must be able to withstand such torture tests without great harm.

■ The knife is an indispensable survival tool for the individual fighter: Cutting open a deer with the Finnish tactical knife "Puuko."

Photo: Thomas Nohl/Wolfgang Hessler

Cutting through chains
A few years ago, classic metal handcuffs were replaced by so-called "one-way chains" made out of synthetic material. Once they have been put on, they can only be removed by cutting them off. Usually this is accomplished by means of a pair of pliers; if these are not available, knives are often used. In particular, blades with serrated edges are very useful. To be sure, this usage involves a potential risk of injury to the prisoner as well as to the officer himself, as few prisoners act level-headed when they are under arrest and many turn violent.

Cutting through nets
One of the diver's greatest enemies is the fisherman's net. Once trapped in it, only

a knife can help—a vital tool for maritime special forces.

Knives as weapons

Last but not least, knives are also weapons which, depending on the tactical situation, can be used defensively or offensively.

The Role of the Knife According to German Police Regulations
By Bernd Soens

In Germany, national police regulations or the regulations for the national border patrol determine how local police officers can use knives. (Customs and the military have their own regulations.) In carrying out their duties, the police must consider their direct liability first and foremost. This includes their impact on persons or objects through their use of bodily force, equipment and weapons.

The German state of North Rhine-Westphalia has legally defined these concepts and enumerated which weapons are authorized. The weapons include billy clubs, pistols, revolvers, shotguns and submachine guns and this list is identical for every German state except for Bavaria, which also lists machine guns and hand grenades. Therefore, knives are not permitted as weapons and can only be used to assist in the officer's use of bodily force. A non-comprehensive list of these aids includes items such as handcuffs, water cannons, service dogs, service horses, service vehicles, etc., but knives are not included. If knives can be classified, they can only be classified as aids.

The lawmakers consciously made the weapons list comprehensive because of the special purpose of weapons. However, this list only makes sense if the definition of a weapon is precise. Otherwise, an object that is defined here as a weapon can be used as an aid. For this reason, determining what an object is must revolve around the definition of a weapon. If an object fulfills the conceptual characteristics of a weapon according to German law, it must be expressly regulated by law. Then, it cannot be included among the aids to bodily force.

According to German law, if knives were officially forbidden because they are classified as beating and stabbing weapons, then this would also include combat and diver's knives. Knives are intentionally not classified as weapons; otherwise the lawmakers would have included them in the list. Today it is well known that members of the special forces and diving units are equipped with knives. Following the previous argument, these knives may be carried but not used. Merely carrying these knives

The author is head police commissioner and was employed for over 17 years for with the SEK in Cologne, including as training leader for the SEK in North Rhine-Westphalia.

■ **Door opener: A member of the Canadian special force commando ERT demonstrates a classic action scenario with a "TAC Custom" made by knifemaker Wally Hayes.**

Photo: Wally Hayes/Norm Goulet

presents no legal breach. It is scarcely imaginable that these knives should be supplied only for logistical use and not for anything else. It is logically comprehensible that a diver might cut himself free without infringing on the rights of others. But, for example, if a door is crow-barred open, this immediately becomes the use of force against an object—using a weapon. Similarly, if a police officer finds an urgent need for an attack dog to be quickly eliminated, this falls under the same category.Although using a knife in certain deployment situations is urgently necessary, clearly the lawmakers did not want this to be interpreted according to the definition. But then the question arises as to how it should be legally explained and classified.

First of all, we must look at weapons regulations in terms of general exemptions and authorizations. German law, which describes the areas of authorized use and exceptions to weapons regulations, states in part:

This law does not apply to the highest state and federal authorities, the *Bundeswehr* and the *Deutsche Bundesbank,* including their agents, insofar as they are acting within their official capacity, unless otherwise indicated. This applies to police penal system officers and customs officials carrying out police penal system duties, insofar as they are empowered by their official orders, as well as for using officially supplied firearms to carry out acts of force and carrying such firearms outside of their official duties.

Note that in this paragraph only firearms are listed, but not beating and stabbing weapons. There is no general exemption for beating and stabbing weapons. In spite of this legal description, according to police regulations, this enumeration of the right to carry weapons does not provide for a general exception to the regulations of the weapons laws. A switchblade with a two-sided sharpened blade is just as illegal in the hands of a police officer on duty as it is in the hands of a private citizen.

According to police regulations and weapons laws, the mere carrying of officially assigned permissible knives by police officers on duty is irrelevant because there is no intrusion on rights. However, the questions of whether and how knives (not multifunction tools) may be used is legally relevant.

According to German law, knives are clearly weapons. However, North Rhine-Westphalia regulations expressly exclude the use of a knife to assist in the use of bodily force, using the definition provided in the weapons laws. But this must have been unintentional, because in certain situations the use of a knife as described is urgently necessary (e.g., divers must cut themselves free from ropes and SEK officers must crowbar open a window). If at all possible, the immediate use of force can be legalized only for temporary situations. Accordingly, an agency that supplies a knife to an officer does so with the understanding that it may only be used as a tool and only as a tool, without exception. Of course, defenses like self-defense and emergency provide justification for the use of bodily force.

Today many police officers carry privately purchased knives on duty. Merely carrying such knives can be considered a violation of the law. The situation can become especially critical if the officer exercises immediate force with his knife. The weapons laws will probably apply in full force because this knife was not officially supplied within the line of duty.

Using knives by exercising immediate force obviously opens a number of legal questions. In my opinion, police officers are well advised to avoid using privately obtained knives on duty when exercising immediate force, even against objects.

Commando Special Forces (Kommando Spezialkräfte)

The *Kommando Spezialkräfte* (Commando Special Forces, "KSK") are special military forces belonging to the *Bundeswehr*. The establishment of these special forces was prompted by the serious unrest and massacres in Rwanda in 1994. At that time, the German government had to ask its NATO partner Belgium for military assistance in rescuing German citizens from the small African country. In order to be able to adequately react to similar crises in the future using its own forces, the *Bundeswehr* officially established the KSK in 1996. By April 1997, the first troops reported for duty at the garrison of Calw, in the northern Black Forest.

■ **The exclusive choice of the KSK: The burnished Gerber "Mark II" model (above) and the Böker special design "A-F Black" with PVC-coated surface.**

The immediate responsibilities of the KSK include:

• Extracting vital information in crisis and conflict areas.

• Protecting their own forces from a distance and individuals in particular locations.

• Rescuing and evacuating German citizens and/or other persons in certain locations abroad.

■ **Always handy: Classic knife-carrying method in the KSK; on the thigh belt of the pistol pouch.**

• Engaging in combat missions in enemy territory.

This broad spectrum of responsibilities entails supplying special equipment to the soldiers. Besides a number of modern weapons and equipment, a tactical knife completes the uniform. From the beginning it was clear that neither the old *Bundeswehr* combat knife nor the former NVA's converted combat knife "Schwer" was appropriate. At first, primarily based on its classic military applications, the Gerber model "Mark II," with its black burnished L-6 carbon steel blade—partially serrated on both edges—was chosen. The "Mark II" was carried in a Cordura sheath, which could only be fastened on a few parts of the body because of a shortage of optional fasteners. It just made sense to fasten the knife to the belt or on the front of the thigh. For this, the sheath's loop was simply attached to the leg belt of the tactical pistol holster or magazine pouch. Alternatively, the knife could be carried also in the combat vest that was made especially for the KSK. A pocket running diagonally contained the sheath.

However, the Calw soldiers came to the relatively quick conclusion that the "Mark II" could not adequately fulfill their needs. For this reason, a new market search was carried out in 1997 and the available tactical knives were tested. The newly manufactured "Applegate-Fairbairn" knife, which was brought out in the same year by the Solingen company Böker, was close to being ideal. However, Böker had to adapt the knife to the special demands of the KSK. Among the special characteristics of this unique model was a black coating on all metal parts. After the KSK rejected a Teflon coating, which was, to be sure, inexpensive but rubbed off too easily, they decided on a hard coating of titanium aluminum nitrite. The manufacturer took the greatest care with the handle because brass could only be coated semi-permanently. To make matters worse, it turned out that the handle kept rubbing against the Kydex sheath locking mechanism (the Kydex sheath itself fit the KSK's needs and they did not want that changed). The eventual solution was to have the handle made out of steel, which was then covered with an extremely scratch-resistant titanium aluminum nitrite coating.

The "A-F Black" knife, as Böker called it, has a blade of 440-C steel. The Solingen company did offer a less expensive alternative made out of 1.4034 steel, but the Calw experts placed a higher priority on a greater cutting ability. The Kydex sheath, made exclusively by the American Kydex specialists Blade Tech, also complied with the latest tactical demands. Using this sheath, the blade is optimally cared for and protected during parachuting and rapelling because of the sheath's extremely resilient material. Injuries to the wearer can pretty much be ruled out. The sheath contains two locking mechanisms that secure the knife very well. Several ring loops also permit the sheath to be easily attached to different pieces of equipment.

Besides this tactical knife, a multipurpose tool also is part of the KSK soldier's equipment. Just as the other special forces did, the KSK chose Leatherman's "Super Tool."

■ **KSK members adopt an initial position. The kneeling soldier carries his Gerber "Mark II" on the left thigh.**
Photo: BMVg

Border Protection Squadron 9 (Grenzschutzgruppe 9)

■ **Alternative carrying method in a specially designed pocket of the KSK combat vest.**

Photo: BMVg

On September 5, 1972, during the summer Olympic games in Munich, members of the Palestinian terrorist group "Black September" attacked the Israeli team in the Olympic Village. After they had killed two athletes, they took the rest as hostages and demanded helicopters, which they planned to bring to the airport at Fürstenfeldbruck. From there they wanted to board a waiting airplane and fly to Egypt. At the airport, Bavarian police officers were already waiting to rescue the hostages. Because this form of violent terrorism in Germany was as yet unknown and the police were neither trained nor equipped with the proper weapons for that kind of situation, the rescue effort ended in tragedy: all of the hostages died. In reaction to this, the Ministry of the Interior decided to establish a unit to fight terrorism as well as the most violent criminal acts. The focus fell to the border patrol, which at that time was divided into eight squadrons. The newly established special unit was likewise considered a squadron and was consequently given the moniker *Grenzschutzgruppe 9* (Border Protection Squadron 9, "GSG 9"). The first commander of the squadron, Ulrich K. Wegener, was astoundingly successful in establishing the unit, and just five years later, the GSG 9 proved their strike power by storming the hijacked Lufthansa airplane "Landshut" in Mogadishu.

The GSG 9 is one of the leading anti-terrorism groups worldwide. The group ensures that their arms and equipment feature the very latest developments in order to most effectively carry out their duties. For their first set of supplies, the GSG 9 had a combat knife that was introduced in the *Bundeswehr* in 1968. This simple knife included a conical sharpened blade, a synthetic handle, and a traditional aluminum sheath that closed with a latch. Although the *Bundeswehr* described it as a combat knife, the GSG 9 could not describe it as such or use it as a weapon due to legal reasons (see Bernd Soens' article on page 59). Therefore, just two weeks after its official introduction, the combat knife

■ Insignia of the Grenzschutzgruppe 9.

was renamed "work knife," which in any case better describes how it was used by within the GSG 9. First and foremost the knife was used as a tool and it had to serve for the most diverse jobs, whether for cutting ropes, as a screwdriver or as a crowbar. It was even sometimes used for digging, because terrorists belonging to the so-called *Roten Armee Fraktion* (Red Army Fraction, "RAF") would hide their weapons caches in the German forests. Until the end of the 1970s, the GSG 9 kept this knife as part of their standard equipment.

Parallel to this, Puma introduced its "Auto-Allzweck-Messer" in 1973, but only special squadron leaders, precision gunners and members of the technical unit carried it. The technical unit of the GSG 9 was responsible for supporting the storm troops through diversionary tactics as well as defusing bombs and explosive devices. The design advantages of the "Auto-Allzweck-Messer" as opposed to the "Bundeswehr-Kampfmesser" were twofold and allowed it to be used for additional jobs: the sharpened hatchet edge on the rear of the blade and the slight dovetailing on the rear third of the blade. Because it gave excellent protection during general hitting and cutting while securing the soldier's position, as well as being effective for cutting cables and wires during bomb defusements, this knife proved to be clearly superior to all others. Even two decades later, some members of the GSG 9 still use the "Auto-Allzweck-Messer."

In the late 1970s, the "Feldmesser 78" came into favor after its introduction by the Austrian company Glock, which would later achieve great international success with its polymer grip-equipped "Glock 17."

■ Below: GSG 9 knives since 1973: Puma "Auto-Allzweck" knife; Glock "Bundeswehrmesser 78" and "Feldmesser 78" in black and olive models.

At that time the "Glock-Feldmesser" was one of the most groundbreaking innovations on the steel weapons market insofar as its design, locking technology, and sheath and handle material were concerned. Without a doubt, it can be called one of the first tactical knives. The body of the sheath, the knife locking mechanism and the belt loops consist of single die-cast parts. The belt loop can be opened by one simple motion and offers additional attachment possibilities to other objects such as combat vests, thigh belts for pistol holsters and magazine pouches, or backpacks. The first edition came completely blackened with rear serration, followed

■ **Right: First supplied in 1973: GSG 9 officer during an attack drill with a "Bundeswehr-Kampfmesser" on his belt.**

■ **GSG 9 officer in 2001 with a Glock "Feldmesser 78" worn upside-down on his tactical vest.**

by a standard olive-colored model with a flat blade back. Today the black models are found exclusively in the equipment of the second combat unit of the GSG 9 (divers), while the standard model is carried by all other members of the GSG 9. Despite its advantages, the "Glock-Feldmesser" does, however, have certain clear drawbacks. Because the blades are made from burnished carbon steel, it is not very resistant to rust and the damaged surfaces are often found fault with damaged. In addition, it does not have a very great cutting ability.

All four of these knife models are still found today within the arsenal of the GSG 9.

As with all the other special forces, in the mid-1990s the multifunction tool took hold in the GSG 9. However, it is officially supplied only to the technical unit and the paratroopers of the 3rd combat unit. While the technical unit preferred Victorinox's "Swiss Tool," the paratroopers decided on Gerber's "Woodsman" with a deployable metal saw. Most of the other members of the GSG 9 equip themselves privately with multifunction tools from various manufacturers, just like their colleagues in the SEKs. It is certainly more expensive for the individual to buy his own model, but this does have an advantage in that he is able to get choose the model that best suits his needs.

Police special forces (Spezialeinsatzkommandos & Mobilen Einsatzkommandos)

Because of the federal system in Germany, police matters lie within the sovereignty of the individual states. Managing police situations with a high potential for endangerment (e.g., the taking of hostages, blackmail, and kidnappings) falls within the jurisdiction of the state police. As a logical result of this, each state established its own special unit. To fight the most serious crimes, the *Spezialeinsatzkommandos* (Special Assignment Commandos, "SEK") and the *Mobilen Einsatzkommandos* (Mobile Assignment

Commandos, "MEK") were established. While the SEK is mostly used for any kind of emergency mission, the MEK's focus is on surveillance. Because every state has its own special units, each with its own different weaponry and equipment, this section will focus on the tactical knives used by the SEK units in North Rhine-Westphalia and Hesse.

With the establishment of the first SEKs in Dortmund, Düsseldorf and Cologne, knives already were part of the officers' equipment. Just as with the GSG 9, the decision to include a knife in one's personal arsenal was in the early years less due to tactical considerations than from the concept that special combat forces should, in principle, also have knives at their disposal. The knife was regarded first and foremost as an ersatz toolbox that should always be carried on one's person. Multifunction tools, which are available on the market today, did not yet exist and were unavailable to the GSG 9 and SEKs. Thus, knives were commonly misused as screwdrivers and crowbars. And it was precisely because of this that the first model that was chosen was completely unsuitable. The North Rhine-Westphalia SEK chose for its first service model the "White Hunter" from the Solingen company Puma (but with a wood handle shell instead of the usual horn).

(The name "White Hunter" actually refers to the African professional hunters and

■ The knives of the Nordrhein-Westphalien Westphalian SEK: the Weber "SEK" (top) and the Puma "White Hunter" with wooden handle.

■ Right: SEK officer in the 1970s cutting a plug lead with the Puma "White Hunter."

expedition hunters for big game. It does conjure up allusions to its use by hunters in Africa. It is an interesting fact that the elite South African Reconnaissance Commandos, "Recces" for short, used to carry this knife as a "bush tool." Once they were trained and gained some combat experience, they were—and are—some of the best special combat troops in the world.)

This heavy hunting knife was chosen after a search among the available models in the early 1970s, and was thought to be fully appropriate according to the understanding of the time. However, its failings first became apparent when it was misused as a tool: when used as a crowbar, the blade regularly broke off because of the relatively narrow, flat handle infrastructure. Also, the comfort of the handle left much to be desired; the wood handle shell was not voluminous enough to adequately fill the hand. Finally, the replacement cost for the heavy hunting knife was rather high (for the police to procure, mind you, not for the ministers and ministry officials!).

A classic use of this knife as a tool is related by a former officer of the Cologne SEK: "During a highly calculated search for a wanted violent criminal we were combing through a forested area, when suddenly we got word that the perpetrator had been

■ Below: Used by the Nordrhein-Westphalian SEK since the 1980s—the model "SEK" from the Rudolf Weber, Jr. company.

The "Amphibian"—Knife as Lifesaver
By Jürgen Sohnemann

The strike force approaches a bridge on the Rhine, 496 river kilometers high. Everything looks normal: a couple of seagulls screeching over the brown, rushing water and cargo boats transporting scrap metal, oil and gravel towards the Netherlands. It is late morning on a beautiful August day when the "hostage taker" puts down his telescope and, grinning broadly, turns to his bound victim on the floor and the ship's captain. An "FN High Power" is sticking out of his waistband. He certainly has nothing to fear…

The strike force passes a fixed shore marker and the leader of the special commando unit starts the countdown: "3 – 2 – 1 – Go!" When the strike force ship's forecastle is engulfed in the shadow of the bridge, some heavily armed masked men emerge from the dark steel structure and glide spider-like down ropes towards the deck, while from the rear, speedboats carrying additional SEK forces race up to the target ship.

Two men from the commando unit have already loosened themselves from their ropes on the deck and storm towards the helm with their weapons ready. The "criminal"—who is occupied with the radio—has not yet noticed the imminent disaster, as this drill turns into a serious situation. So as not to collide with a small structure on the upper deck, team members 3 and 4 stop short to touch down closer to the cabin on the deck. The delay takes a few seconds longer than expected, for the pendulous motion of the rope soon disappears at the landing point. The third man touches down, shortly before number 4. Already dangerously close to the cabin, number 4's rope, which is fastened to the bridge up above, gets caught on the roof and becomes taut. Freeing himself from the rapelling apparatus is impossible!

After landing against the taut rope, number 4 is immediately snatched up into the air again, collides with the cabin's deck rail and is catapulted another three meters upward. At the very last second, number 3 succeeds in ripping his Kershaw "Amphibian" out of the front pocket of his leg holster and slicing through the taut rope with one quick slash. From about three meters in the air, number 4 drops onto the afterdeck, hits his helmeted head on a capstan, goes overboard and disappears in the rear current of the tug boat….

Immediately calls go out over the radio: "Man overboard! Stop your boats!" and "Aborted drill—rescue mission!" But even before these announcements, the water safety police captains who witnessed the event react without hesitation.

Rescue forces close off the scene of the accident. Seconds turn into an eternity, until the seemingly lifeless body, wrapped in a protective vest, appears out of the brown

The author has been employed by the Frankfurt SEK for 17 years.

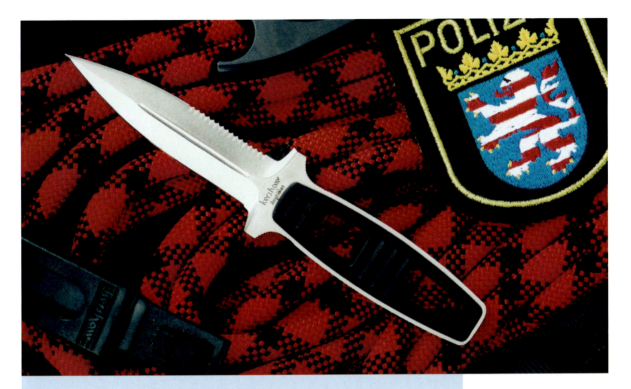

water many meters downstream. At the ambulance he is diagnosed with several wounds to the head and torso and a fractured forearm. His comrades use their tactical knives to cut open his clothing.

After just a few weeks, the officer is able to resume his duties in spite of a few teeth being lost, his lower arm being fractured, a concussion and numerous other wounds. In light of these circumstances, unit member number 3 cannot say with certainty whether his small double-edged knife actually saved his comrade's life, but he can say with certainty that it kept him from being even more severely injured!

This situation illustrates some considerations that played a decisive role in the acquisition of the "Amphibian" tactical knife:
• The knife must be of a "portable" weight and size.
• Its sharpness and shape must be appropriate for use as a tool as well as a weapon.
• It must be able to be fastened securely to combat gear to keep it from getting lost.
• It should not matter which side of the blade is used.
• The knife must be attached to an easily accessible part of the gear so that, through practice drills and actual missions, it can be accessed automatically.

Together with some other important considerations, the above-described event had a positive effect in that it was never again questioned whether the Frankfurt SEK should carry tactical knives and the main concern became which knife to carry.

■ Lifesaver! Kershaw's "Amphibian," used by the Hessian SEK in Frankfurt, saved an officer from life-threatening injuries during an attack drill.

located. We immediately moved in the specified direction and saw an obstacle in the form of a barbed wire fence. We took our [Puma] knives and immediately dug ourselves through under the fence."

In 1985, the procurement authorities for the Cologne SEK took the initiative to search for an appropriate successor for the Puma "White Hunter." They struck gold with the International Weapons Exhibition (IWA) in Nürnberg. The Rudolf Weber, Jr. company showed itself responsive to the special demands of the SEK. At least at that point in time, one can speak about the first tactical considerations that were given to this brand-new knife. First of all, it had to have much more stable handle than the "White Hunter" to be able to withstand the enormous demands placed upon it by being used as a crowbar. Second, a serrated back edge was designed that would increase the knife's utility as a tool. In addition, a small ripping, serrated edge on the rear third of the blade was requested for easy cutting of belts and ropes (which, it is true, the "White Hunter" already had). The most important requirement, however, had to do with the handle: it needed to be larger in diameter and be made out of a rustproof synthetic material instead of wood, so that it could be grasped more comfortably and securely in the hand.

Rudolf Weber, Jr. used the extant *Bundeswehr-Pilotenmesser* as the basis for these requests and changed the model accordingly. The solution for the handle turned out to be especially interesting in this regard, as it was both inexpensive and effective. The manufacturer heated a special handle made out of synthetic material and pressed it onto the hook-shaped handle infrastructure. The shape of the handle was reminiscent of a carpenter's hammer. The leather sheath was retained, but it was secured by a number of rivets to prevent the blade from sticking through. This knife was officially introduced in 1986. The old Puma knife continued to be used by the special forces until they were unusable and were replaced by the new Weber knives. The Rudolf Weber, Jr. firm still offers its tactical knife today under the name "SEK."

In 1993, the realization sunk in that it was no longer necessary to use a knife as a poor substitute for a tool, because a real tool could be used in the form of the new Leatherman multifunction tools. The diverse tasks that each individual officer had to undertake demanded an original approach. With an unwieldy knife, no one could successfully perform his job without difficulty. Ultimately, the procurement authorities were convinced of the necessity of equipping each individual SEK officer with a multifunction tool. Only then was it guaranteed that in an emergency one could react spontaneously and handle the situation. Thus, in the North Rhine-Westphalia SEK, the knife was gradually replaced, first by the Leatherman multifunction tool "PST," and later by the "Super Tool" model.

Customs Central Support (Zentrale Unterstützungsgruppe Zoll)

In 1997, the increased use of violence by criminals in the area of drug and cigarette smuggling led to the creation of a group of specially trained customs officers who could be called on for support during especially dangerous missions. The training of these officials of the *Zentralen Unterstützungsgruppen Zoll* (Customs Central Support, "ZUZ") and *Zoll-Technik* (Customs Technicians, "ZUZ[T]") took place with the SEKs and the *Fortbildungsstelle für Spezialeinheiten* (Continuing Education Authority for Special Units, "FSE") in the North Rhine-Westphalia cities of Selm and Borg. Local customs investigation departments can request the ZUZ during unusually difficult arrest and surveillance tasks, whereby it corresponds to the SEK in its duties. Even the division of the group was adopted in essence from the SEK. The ZUZ(T) was likewise established for the technical support of regional customs investigation departments. Their division, duties and training can be compared to those of the MEKs. The ZUZ and the ZUZ(T) both belong both to Group 1 (Support Duties) of the *Zollkriminalamt* (Criminal Customs Bureau, "ZKA"), which was established in 1992 as the main federal command.

■ Insignia of the Zentralen Unterstützungsgruppe Zoll-Technik and of the Zentralen Unterstützungsgruppe Zoll (above).

■ The tactical switchblade "Speedlock" from the Böker company is part of the ZUZ and ZUZ(T) officers' equipment.

To be able to handle their duties, these officers needed to be provided with modern weapons and equipment, just as with all the other special forces branches. Because the ZUZ and the ZUZ(T) were entirely new units, they did not need to revert to

■ ZUZ(T) troops with Böker "Speedlock" knives worn in cases horizontally on their belts.

■ The ZUZ and ZUZ(T) also wear the Cordura case on the vertical leg belt of their pepper spray holsters.

existing and possibly worn-out older equipment, but could inspect the latest technology to find equipment that corresponded to their needs. Besides the obligatory "Super Tool" by Leatherman, a tactical knife was also chosen. The customs units preferred a switchblade that could be used one-handed, to a knife with a fixed blade. Special value was given to a partially serrated edge. Among the limited selection was the Böker "Speedlock" model with a matte chrome aluminum body and sand-flecked blade. After a preliminary test of various knives, the ZUZ and ZUZ(T) finally decided on this model, which at that point was still equipped with a 1.4034 steel blade. Later, in the year 2000, another version was made especially for the ZUZ utilizing an ATS-34 steel blade with a serrated edge, which had a much greater cutting ability. The "Speedlock" is carried in the original Cordura case supplied by Böker, and can be carried horizontally as well as vertically. The officers of the ZUZ and ZUZ(T) fasten their cases—according to their individual duties—either horizontally on the belt or vertically on the leg belt of the pistol holster, that is, the carrying system for chemical repellents. The ZUZ and ZUZ(T) thus belong to the few special forces around the world that are officially supplied with a tactical switchblade.

■ The ZUZ and ZUZ(T) cannot do without their multifunction tools. Here, the "Super Tool" model from the Leatherman company.

Folding Tactical Knives

F olding knife, or knife with a fixed blade? This question can only be answered in connection with the tactical use. Which tasks must the knife be able to undertake in combat? Can it be open in a sheath or must it be concealed? Folding knives have the advantage over knives with fixed blades in that they are smaller in size when closed and therefore can be hidden more easily from prying eyes. The advantage of knives with fixed blades, on the other hand, lies in their greater stability and more secure handling. The following description of both types of knives is, therefore, wholly unbiased.

For many years folding knives were regarded as rather inappropriate in the area of combat knives, except for the famous parachute-cutting knife of the German *Luftwaffe* in WWII and its British counterpart (as well as the *Bundeswehr* copy). These reservations were mostly based on the fact that the locking mechanisms were insufficient and the knife could not be used with one hand. However, over the years all that has changed. A number of technically sophisticated locking systems means that the blade can be made to be maximally resilient without the user's having to fear that it will accidentally open and

■ Heavy artillery—deluxe handmade tactical knives, from left: ".458 Magnum" (Greg Lightfoot), "Mod. 4" (Harold Carson), "Kasper" (Pat Crawford) and "Oracle" (Allen Elishewitz).

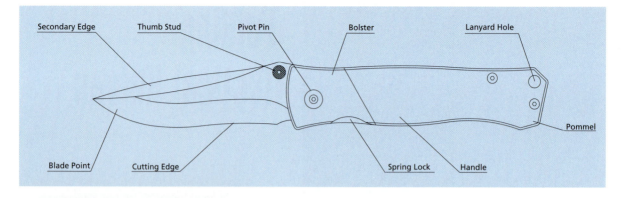

Secondary Edge | Thumb Stud | Pivot Pin | Bolster | Lanyard Hole

Blade Point | Cutting Edge | Spring Lock | Handle | Pommel

■ **Above: The parts of a folding tactical knife.**

■ **Left: The first tactical knife with a spring locking mechanism, Michael Walker's "Liner Lock Fighter" from 1983. The mix of materials is the same then as now: the plate is made of titanium, the handle surface of Micarta.**

injure him, i.e., render him unable to fight. Furthermore, on modern knives the blade can be opened with one hand, thanks to the aid of holes, disks and pins. From these folding knives came switchblades, which allow a blade to snap forward or out to the side by means of a spring mechanism. The first one was called "out of the front" ("OTF") in slang terms.

In the United States, the trend toward modern tactical folding knives can be traced back to the latter half of the 1980s. Knifemakers like Bob Terzuola and Pat Crawford first gave the "Combat" and "Tactical Folder" their characteristic appearance, according to today's standards, even though Michael Walker had already introduced his first combat knife ("Liner Lock Fighter") with a spring lock in 1983. Of course, before that time other manufacturers had already employed certain modern elements— for example, the mechanics of one-handed blade opening, the use of titanium as a handle material or equipping their knives with trouser clips—but only now did combining all these elements lead to the new phenotype. In the mid-1990s, another stylistic element appeared in the "Chisel Grind" model: a chisel-shaped ground Tanto blade. Knifemaker Ernest Emerson deserves the credit for this by making the Tanto flick folding popular through clever marketing. Companies like Spyderco and Benchmade recognized early on the potential that lay behind these handmade knives and immediately engaged successful knife manufacturers to design them. Today it is the rare tactical folding knife that comes on the market that was not designed by a well-known knifemaker or a hand-to-hand combat expert. Names and philosophies are indispensable tools for marketing within the knife industry.

Tactical switchblades are also emphasized in the development of modern folding knives. They owe their existence and broad distribution to the increased use of computer controlled production plants, which first made mill-cut handle parts out of aluminum according to technical specifications for parts with minimal tolerances. The undisputed leader in this market is Micro Tech, which continued to raise the bar with its technical innovations. Although the demand for these high-tech knives is great, the supply remains limited, because of the high price the customer has to fork out for these extravagantly made knives.

Despite these brilliant technical developments, the appearance of tactical folding knives has remained essentially unchanged in recent years. One-handed blades generally appear in unremarkable gray or black and have a serrated edge on the rear third of the blade. They are usually shaped like a modified Bowie, spear, drop point, or Tanto (for further discussion of blade shapes, see page 145). As far as the handles are concerned, aluminum, titanium, carbon fiber, Micarta, G-10 or fiberglass-strengthened artificial materials like Zytel, i.e., Grilon, have gained

■ **Bob Terzuola and Pat Crawford's pioneering designs served as models for these tactical folding knives (manufacturers, from top): Mission Knives (MPF), Blade Tech, Warren Osborne, Walter Brend and Chris Reeve (Sebenza).**

■ Left: Ernest Emerson brought the chisel-shaped ground blade into fashion among tactical knives. Top, Benchmade's "CQC 7"; bottom, the "Specwar" model from Emerson's own workshop.

■ Below: Modern tactical folding knives with Tanto blades and fiberglass-enhanced polyamide, G-10 and aluminum 6061-TS handles. From left: "Gunsite" (Cold Steel), "Bob Lum" (Spyderco), "CUDA" (Camillus), "SOCOM" (Micro Tech) and "M-16" (Columbia River Knife & Tool).

acceptance. Quick access to the knife is generally ensured by a trouser clipA trouser clip generally ensures quick access to the knife. Knives that are carried exclusively in cases are rare. Regarding locking systems, manufacturers overwhelmingly rely on the "Liner Lock" or the "Lock Back." In contrast to fixed-blade knives, it is less logical to distinguish among folding knives according to their specific areas of use. Hence, in the following sections, the distinction drawn will be between manually opened one-handed knives and switchblades.

One-handed knives

The hallmark of the tactical folding is the one-handed hold. The knife must be able to be accessed in a matter of seconds, and only with one hand. Gone are the days when, in opening a folding knife, one hand gripped the handle and the other pulled out the blade by means of the fingernails.

Two names are tightly associated with the one-handed folding knife. The first is Spyderco, which in 1981 issued and patented its "Worker" model with a hole in the blade that created a one-handed system. The company's founder, Sal Glesser, experimented with various opening mechanisms, but he finally settled on the simplest solution: boring a hole into the blade. The second is knifemaker Michael Walker, who decided on a screwed-on pin as an opening mechanism, which is called a "thumb stud" in knifemaking jargon. While earlier manufacturers attached the thumb stud only to one side so that it fit snugly into the half-circle shaped receptacle on the blade unlockingblade-unlocking device, modern knives have thumb studs on both sides. That way the blade can be opened both from the left and from the right—which is logical. However, this presupposes that the thumb stud is attached far enough proportionally outside. In addition, care must be taken that the thumb stud is as close as possible on the handle when it is in the open position so that it is not a hindrance while cutting. Knifemaker Butch Valloton provided an elegant solution to this problem by fastening the thumb stud directly to the handle and using it simultaneously as an impact pin for locking the blade.

■ **Characteristic of the tactical folding knife is that its blade can be opened with one hand.**

Another alternative to the pin as blade raiser is a small milled disk, familiar from on compasses. This is screwed onto the back of the blade and the blade raised on either side by means of both the half-circles. Knifemaker Bob Terzuola is generally recognized as the father of this system. Adopting this idea, Terzuola's Canadian colleague Brian Tighe installed a right-angled blade raiser on his knives. In the end,

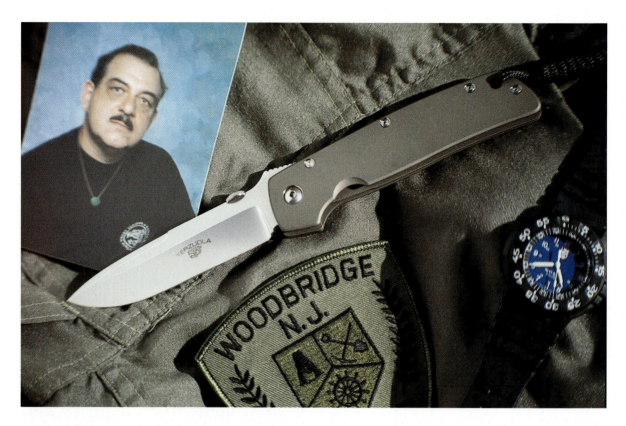

Bob Terzuola's "ATCF" shows the typical appearance of tactical folding knives in the late 1980s.

though, it does not matter what the blade raiser looks like, only that both sides must be usable and the blade raiser should not extend too far into the middle of the blade.

The easiest way of dealing with the whole problem is to bore a hole in the blade à la Spyderco. Many knife companies, including Gerber, Benchmade and SOG, choose this method for certain models, even if they have to pay a licensing fee to Spyderco. Knives without an opening aid can be refitted with "The Stud." This simple blade raiser is simply placed on the back of the blade and affixed by means of an interior six-sided screw. Of course, there are still other opening mechanisms for blades, but they have not really caught on in the tactical field. Emerson Knives and Camillus have found more success with alternative opening mechanisms. Knifemaker Ernest Emerson has patented an opening mechanism for his "Commander" model that can be anchored to the trouser pocket—the blade opens up simultaneously as the knife is being pulled out. However, sturdy trouser material and some practice are necessary. Camillus developed the "CUDA," a knife whose blade can be opened entirely without pins, disks or holes. A milled plate protrudes from the handle surface and is attached tightly to the blade. When the thumb pushes the little plate along the front edge, the fingers force the blade open.

The same abundance of ideas that are found in opening mechanisms are also found in locking systems. Names like "Liner Lock," "Lock Back," "Axis Lock,"

"Compression Lock," "Rolling Lock," "ARC-Lock," "Button Lock," "Blade Lock," and "Discovery Lock," are only some of those currently existing on the American market, and many of these specialized ideas are protected by copyright. The overwhelming majority of all tactical folding knives are outfitted, then as now, with "Liner Locks" or "Lock Backs." With the "Lock Back," the tip of a springed lever pushes into a gap in the rear of the blade. The unlocking lever can be found either farther back on the blade or in the middle. With some practice, the lever can be pressed in the middle without having to grope around for it. However, the other hand is needed to close the blade in a controlled manner. Here we see the advantage of the "Liner Lock" system, which is based entirely on a one-handed principle.

With the "Liner Lock," a liner sits on one side of the handle, springs forward upon opening and attaches to the blade from beneath. To close the liner, it is simply pushed back with the thumb and the blade is closed with the thumb and forefinger. The second purpose of the liner is to secure the blade in a closed position. This is accomplished by a small steel ball that fits precisely into a hole or an indentation in the blade. In general, liners are made of stainless steel or titanium. In order to avoid the danger of accidentally pushing the liner, most modern folding knives forego large thumb moldings. More often, manufacturers ensure that the liner is not allowed to project over the underside of the handle. The liner and handle surfaces are flush with one another. Milling generally ensures a firm grip on the liner.

The liner developed by Butch Valloton also offers good safety. He simply bends them in the thumb area and mills them accordingly. Gerber copied this idea for the "Applegate-Fairbairn" folding knife, but simplified it through the use of a separately cast part.

To make the "Liner Lock" even safer, knife makers and manufacturers have invented a range of additional safety parts like "LAWKS" (Lake and Walker Knife Safety Locking System) or "Interlock" (likewise from Lake and Walker), which blocks the liner when it is open.

Based on their lighter weight and simpler cleaning capabilities, most tactical folding knives are designed with an open handle back. In addition, they can be dismantled for larger cleaning jobs, usually by means of an inner six-sided or torque key. However, caution is recommended. Many manufacturers of exclusive brands, like Micro Tech or Masters of Defense, specifically emphasize that they do not like to see their knives dismantled at all, and in certain cases will even void the warranty for doing so. Therefore, the customer should, as when buying medications, study the accompanying packaging very carefully.

■ **Trouser clip: The blade of Emerson's "Commander" opens automatically when pulled out. However, sturdy trouser material and some practice are necessary.**

Another type of one-handed knife is the so-called "fall knife." Gravity allows the blade to fall forward out of the handle. However, this system is clearly not interesting enough to international high-tech knife manufacturers, because people have waited in vain for modern developments and ideas. The Solingen company Eickhorn continues to produce its "Bundeswehr-Fallschirmkappmesser," and since the year 2000 there has also been the model "American Slider," which is sold by the manufacturer of the same name in the United States.

Switchblade knives

In 1987, American knifemaker Ron Miller from Largo, Florida, decided to produce a switchblade knife with a new kind of spring mechanism. He had developed the knife with the ulterior motive of marketing it to the U.S. Army Special Forces Reserve residing in Homestead, Florida. Because Miller could not decide on an appropriate product name, it was simply christened "Black Knife" after its appearance. Early on Miller had already included another Largo knife makerknifemaker, Charles Ochs, in the development process. Ochs gave various suggestions to improve the knife's appearance and handling, and finally took over its marketing because of his strong connections with various special forces. The new-fangled handle managed entirely without a haft, shell or cover. The use of screws rather than rivets simplified its construction and also enabled it to be dismantled simply for the purpose of care or repairs. For locking and unlocking, Miller developed a spring bolt that secured the blade in both positions without either liner or spring lever. At the heart of the switchblade was a spiral projectile spring, which was held in a cut-outcutout groove inside the handle's surface. The knife's construction entailed manufacturing the main components on a computer-controlled milling machine ("CNC"), in order to cut down on the time devoted to making parts by hand as well as the time devoted to assembly. For the handle material Miller selected anodized 6061-T6 aluminum, which is still used today.

Success did not fail to materialize: from 1987 to 1994 Miller made and sold between 8,000 and 10,000 original "Black Knives" in various models. Due to Ochs' connections, most of the knives went to members of special forces and police units. In 1989, the U.S. Navy officially ordered five knives to be tested by the SEALs. By using the somewhat long-winded title "Emergency Chemical, Biological, Radiation Suit Cutter," Ochs wanted to avoid the word "switchblade," which was a negatively loaded term among the U.S. forces. Because at this time the Gulf War was slowly growing more intense and the use of chemical, biological, and radioactive weapons could not be ruled out, the SEALs saw in this one-handed knife an extraordinary tool to free a wounded soldier from his ABC protection suit if necessary. Despite positive reviews, Miller received no official government orders. But apparently that

■ Left: Some examples of various locking systems (from top): "Back Liner" (Bernhard Zwicker), "Axis Lock" (Benchmade), "ARC Lock" (SOG), "Blade Lock" (Columbia River Knife & Tool), "Lock Back" (Spyderco) and "Liner Lock" (Buck).

■ The legendary "Black Knife" started the new wave of switchblades and at the same time was the forerunner of future trends. Here, Charles Ochs' edition.

Photo: Charles Ochs/Point Seven Studios

■ These models from the first wave of tactical switchblades are sought-after classics today (from top): "AFO" (Benchmade), "Brend Fighter" (White Wolf Knives) and "Drop Point Hunter" (White Wolf Knives), all with hand-ground blades from knife maker Walter Brend.

was all the same to the SEALs, because they privately purchased the knife in great quantities. When Miller died in 1995, it looked at first like the "Black Knife" would never again be issued. However, Charles Ochs took control of the situation and began to manufacture them again. Even today he builds somewhat modified versions of the "Black Knife." Besides an additional lengthwise groove cut into the handle, the new models are distinctive from the old models because of an additional trouser clip and serration on the back third of the blade. All the other characteristics of the "Black Knife" remain unchanged. During his lifetime, Miller had neglected to apply for a patent in a timely manner, which ending up having its consequences.

Of course, the rest of the American knife industry soon copied Ochs' lucrative business with tactical switchblades. Just a short time later, the Oregon companies Benchmade and Al Mar introduced a similar model, the "General Purpose Auto" ("GPA"). After its initial success, the knife was later made only by Benchmade and was marketed under the name "Armed Forces Only" ("AFO"). In quick succession the company developed a whole range of switchblades and thus rose to the top of this field, even though legally sales of this knife were only allowed to members of the armed forces and government officials. Most of these models could not be introduced in Germany, because the blades exceeded a length of 8.5 centimeters and were, therefore, contraband according to contemporary German weapons laws.

Besides Benchmade, other smaller firms like White Wolf Knives from North Carolina also offered switchblades, some of which were outfitted with handmade blades. Among the suppliers of these blades was knife makerknifemaker Walter Brend. His limited series was much smaller in quantity than that of Benchmade. Today, "White Wolf" knives with Walter Brend blades are highly sought-after by collectors.

In 1994, the Solingen company Böker was the first European company to introduce a tactical switchblade under the name "Speedlock." (It was designed by the author.) From the beginning, it was foreseen that the handle cover would not be made entirely by CNC milling machines. Rather, the parts would be produced by aluminum casting processes. The advantage was that without the need for additional production time, the side surfaces could be given a single radius, which markedly improved its handling. As a rule, CNC-milled parts have only one flat surface. A clear disadvantage of the press-cast aluminum surfaces was that they could not be anodized. Thus, the surfaces were either satinized by hand or galvanized with a hard coat of chrome. In addition, the innovation of a push button was introduced. Instead of the usual pins, the Solingen company produced a push button that locked flush with the surface. Soon after Böker, another Solingen company, Hubertus, introduced its modern switchblade. In contrast to Böker's "Speedlock," the Hubertus "Z-2000" model contained handle surfaces made of thermoplastic synthetic material.

■ Switchblades from Micro Tech with typical CNC-manufactured 6061-T6 aluminum handles (from top): "M-UDT" (new model), "M-UDT" (old model), "Kestrel" and "Mini-SOCOM."

In 1995, Micro Tech, another Florida manufacturer, presented new switchblade knives to a wide audience. In a very short time, the small company managed to become the market leader in the area of highly specialized tactical switchblades. Their recipe for success: extraordinary designs and individual parts that were made with the highest precision, rivaling the quality of a handmade knife. Besides classic side-opening knives, Micro Tech also relied very strongly on OTF switchblades. Micro Tech is also the uncontested leader here. Micro Tech's collection also emphasized exclusive special models, which arose in collaboration with famous knife makers like Walter Brend. The OTF models "Combat Talon II" and "Nemesis," equipped with hand-ground blades, quickly became classics.

■ **The crowning jewel of Micro Tech's product, the "out of the front" ("OTF") switchblade. The "Nemesis" model (top) and the "Combat Talon II" model have handmade blades from Walter Brend. In the middle, a "Halo III."**

Today a number of manufacturers have proven successful in the area of tactical switchblades, including Masters of Defense, Paragon Knives, Pro-Tech Knives, GT Knives, SWAT Knives and Dalton Knives. After years away from this market, even Al Mar returned to this lucrative business with its models "SERT" and "Auto-SERE," which Paragon was responsible for producing. Thanks to the resourceful knife makerknifemaker Ken Onion, Kershaw even succeeded in developing a switchblade that is legal in nearly all countries of the world. Thanks to his "Speedsafe" system, the switchblade can be opened like a conventional one-handed knife, but after the blade is pushed up to about a third by the thumb, the spring mechanism is activated and the blade automatically springs up. Subsequently, the locking follows over the liner lock.

Another type of switchblade is the so-called dual- or double-action system. Here the user can choose between a one-handed opening or a spring mechanism. The "Chamäleon" model developed by knifemaker Butch Valloton is definitely progressive. Valloton is absolutely considered the pre-eminent authority in the area of switchblades, and he makes his individual pieces entirely by hand. However, there is no rule without an exception: Micro Tech has also issued a CNC-milled "Chamäleon" limited series with aluminum handles. Another brilliant technological success is the dual-action of the "LCC" model,

designed by Canadian knifemaker Greg Lightfoot and manufactured by Micro Tech. Completely lacking a conspicuous push button, the spring mechanism can be activated by pushing the left side.

Modern computer-controlled manufacturing processes allow the realization of ever-more-ambitious ideas, and an end to the developments is not close in sight—to the delight of knife aficionados.

■ **From the very beginning these tactical switchblades from the Masters of Defense company were successful (from top): "CQD," "Tempest," "Hornet," "Trident" and "Ladyhawk."**

Fixed-Blade Tactical Knives

Although in recent years folding knives have made greater and greater advancements in the area of tactical use, it remains undisputed that fixed-blade knives have definite advantages. For one thing, they have greater stability. Considering that police and military knife users use tactical knives overwhelmingly as tools to perform "dirty work," the choice must fall to fixed-blade knives. Modern folding knives can be made with minimal tolerances and their locking systems can be locked firmly into place, but the blade extends behind its pivot point some 5 to 10 mm into the handle. Frankly, it is unlikely that, under normal pressure, the blade will break out of its clasp completely. However, it is possible for the blade to receive clearance, the closing mechanism to loosen and the blade to fold in. Users of knives with solid hafts from beginning

■ As with folding knives, synthetic handle materials and matte surfaces are the rule with fixed-blade knives. The Katz model has a satin finish. From left: "CUDA" (Camillus), "Alley Cat" (Katz), "D2 Bowie" (KA-BAR), D2 Impact (KA-BAR), and bottom, "ATAK II" (Mad Dog).

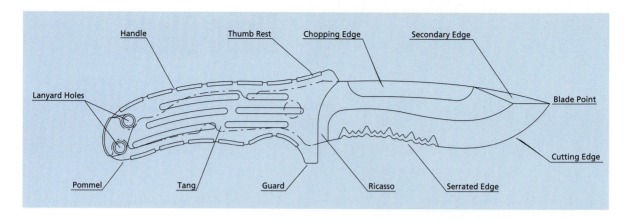

Handle   Thumb Rest   Chopping Edge   Secondary Edge

Lanyard Holes   Blade Point

Cutting Edge

Pommel   Tang   Guard   Ricasso   Serrated Edge

■ **The parts of a fixed-blade knife.**

to end don't have to worry about this. Another, more compelling, argument for this type of knife is the fact that a fixed blade can never fold in on accident. No matter how modern and painstakingly designed, all locking systems and safety devices can never fully ensure that in an extreme situation and under high stress the blade will not inadvertently release. It can happen if one grasps the handle too tight or simply changes his hold on the handle. Modern safety mechanisms as employed by Gerber, Spyderco and Columbia River Knife & Tool, can certainly stop the blade from snapping shut, but once again the main point is that activating this function is time-consuming. It is also questionable whether a user actually is thinking about safety under pressure.

The most persuasive advantage of fixed-blade knives, however, is their greater possibilities of use. In general, blade styles and lengths can be freely chosen and

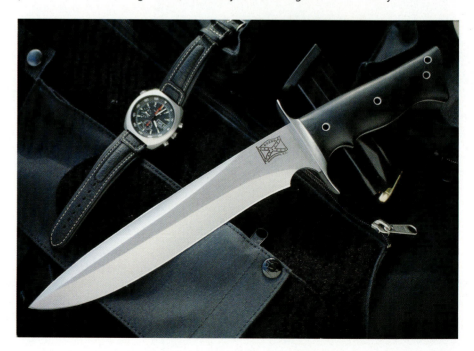

■ **The handmade tactical "Model 2" knife by Walter Brend of South Carolina is characterized by its fantastic craftsmanship.**

do not depend on the length of the handle. With respect to handle materials, certain synthetic materials on fixed-blade tactical knives have become popular, just as with folding knives, if one does not consider the hollow metal of survival knives. Save for a few exceptions, handles are usually black in color. But why one manufacturer chooses to make an extremely hard, shockproof handle out of polycarbonate and another prefers a soft, non-slip rubber is a matter of speculation. Presumably, designers and their expert advisors have different ideas about how a handle is supposed to perform in tactical actions. Both judgments certainly have their logic.

With sheaths as well, modern synthetic materials have almost totally replaced the traditional use of leather. Leather simply has too many disadvantages in terms of its lesser ability to withstand environmental influences like heat, cold, moisture, dirt and violent actions like scratches, sticks and cuts. In contrast, thermoplastic manmade materials or synthetic fibers have proven to be particularly resilient. Tactical users do not simply value sheaths for their durability, but even more for the number of ways they can be carried and attached. With every mission, specialists have to reckon with new situations and carrying methods. One time they have to attach the knife to the combat vest, another time to the thigh or the upper arm. The more attachment options are available, the more useful the knife is.

The following chapter reviews the most important tactical knives with fixed blades. In order to bring some order to this hodgepodge of variations, emphasis will be put on their typical characteristics, common designs and purposes.

General-Purpose Knives

General-purpose fixed-blade knives include those models that reveal no specific tactical function in their size, form, or carrying method. Having a number of functions, they are classic representatives of tactical knives. In spite of their differences, based on their many manufacturers and their various tactical philosophies, some of the characteristics unify them under one type of knife. Because this type of knife is frequently fastened to the body or equipment by a sheath, the blade size averages between 15 and 20 cm. With few exceptions, the blades are gray or black in order to avoid reflectiveness.

Other than blades shaped like daggers, spear points or Bowies, blades shaped like the Japanese Tanto have caught on the most. American knifemaker Phil Hartsfield even went one step further (i.e., one step into the past), in that he ground his Tanto blade on only one side, similar to a carpenter's chisel. This characteristics was already found on early Japanese combat knives. Ernest Emerson, who uses this cut on his folding knives, also designed his fixed-blade Tantos similarly. Together with Timberline's head designer, Vaughn Neely, Emerson developed under the name "Specwar" the first industrially made combat knife with his typical Tanto blade. Often manufacturers market the deep-penetrating

■ Above: Tanto blades have formed the phenotype of tactical knives for a long time (from left): "Tsunami" (SOG)," "Specwar" (Timberline), "Recon Tanto" (Cold Steel) and "Black Tanto" (KA-BAR).

■ Left: The knife maker Wally Hayes developed the "TAC Custom" model for the Canadian special forces, the ERT.

action of this blade shape; this claim is especially popular in connection with Kevlar bullet-proofbulletproof vests. The fact is, however, that Kevlar vests can *not* be penetrated by the Tanto blade. It is different for a blade with a smaller cross-section, for example a dagger blade or even an ice pick. But even if this dubious claim is overlooked, the Tanto blade does have enormous stability as opposed to other shapes. However, Cold Steel and the knifemaker Tom Johanning feel themselves drawn to the traditional Tanto blade that is ground on two sides. Johanning's models "TAC 10" and "TAC 11" can withstand the most grueling tests because of their extremely sturdy Tanto blades.

Besides the Tanto blade, other traditional forms for tactical knives have caught on. Many professional users place greater value on the multiple functions of a blade than on a massive

■ Right: These handmade knives by Tom Johanning ("TAC 11") and Stefan Steigerwald (left) are supremely resilient because of the way in which they were built as fully integrated, stable units.

■ Below: Representing Scandinavia. Above, P. J. Peltonen's version of the traditional Finnish "Puuko." Below, the Fällkniven "A-1," which is not just used by the Swedish military.

blade point with great penetrating power. A good example of this is the "ATAK," developed by Mad Dog, or the "Special Operations Knife" from the Dutch knife manufacturer Hill Knives, both of which are equipped with rather bulbous "drop point" blades.

Modified dagger or "spear point" blades likewise can be found among tactical knives. The model "D2 Impact" from KA-BAR should be mentioned here as an example. But even after nearly two centuries, Bowie blades have not become

obsolete. KA-BAR makes its classic WWII Bowie combat knife in a modernized form, suitable for tactical use. The Swedish knife manufacturer Fällkniven likewise hearkens back to the Bowie blade with its model "A-1." Swiss knife manufacturer Klötzli produces a truly unusual blade form for a tactical knife. This dagger-shaped ground blade narrows into a point and can thus be used as a screwdriver. Moreover, the danger of injury during free cutting is thereby minimized.

In conclusion, it can be said that the Tanto blade was the forerunner in the field of tactical knives. Market surveys show, however, that most manu-facturers and users prefer to be true to conventional blade shapes, even if they are often modified. Most models—like folding knives—have a blade whose rear third is partially serrated or toothed to enable ropes and belts to be cut through quickly.

■ The Vienna knife specialist "Der Messerkönig" created this patented model "JAGKO" at the special request of a soldier in the Jagdkommando, the special forces of the Austrian army.

Maritime Knives

For knives that are meant for maritime use, there are very specific requirements with respect to shape, material and carrying possibilities. For armed divers, the use of knives as tools is much more significant than for all other tactical users because—other than James Bond—there are hardly any documented cases in which two enemy divers have engaged in a knife fight under water.

A tactical diver's knife must meet the following requirements. First of all, the blade should be long enough to be able to cut through ropes, belts, tubes and nets. A serration on the rear third of the blade is standard, as with all general-purpose tactical knives. As opposed to knives carried by sport divers, the tactical blade must be inflexible. Very brightly polished blades certainly are more rustproof and can be found more easily underwater, but they can also betray armed divers by reflecting at night. Opinions among combat swimmers, divers and minelayers, as well as manufacturers, differ as to two other characteristics of the blade. Some insist on serration on the back of the blade, as with earlier diver's knives. Others claim that if the bottom edge is serrated, one can easily accomplish one's duties, and moreover, it is possible to exert additional force on the back of the blade with one's hand. The same goes for the ripping hook. For some it is indispensable for

■ Not only the military, but also police special forces with maritime duties carry knives with corrosion-proof blades—here, the "SK-T" model by the Seaman Subs company.
Photo: HSS International

■ **Carrying the knife on the diving vest ensures quick access. This is the Böker "Orca" model which was designed by Bernd Soens and the author.**

cutting through nets, the nemesis of divers underwater; for others, it is totally useless, because when pulling on the cutting surface of the hook, the net does not offer the right resistance. Only rarely are nets fastened tautly in two places; usually they drift freely in the water.

As with general-purpose tactical knives, individual manufacturers and their designers and advisors have different priorities, and they work these into their products.

Nevertheless, the following points are indisputable: the size of the blade should be as small as possible so that it can be easily gripped with wet suit gloves. Also, the handle should be shaped so that it will fit correctly in the hand on the first grip. If underwater for a long time, the body gradually cools down and control over motor functions becomes increasingly more difficult. A grip belt secures the knife in the hand, for if a diver loses his knife underwater, it could in some circumstances mean death. Artificial material sprayed onto the haft has gained general acceptance as handle material, and sometimes it is strengthened by fiberglass or Kevlar. The spray guarantees an insoluble union of handle and blade that won't crack.

The total length of the knife, however, cannot exceed a certain point. Specifically for armed divers, it is important they be able to carry their knives on as many parts of the body as possible. Attaching knives to the underarm, i.e., the upper arm, or to the chest area of the diving vest is popular. This allows the diver in danger the quickest access under specific circumstances. Also, the diver can see the knife on his arm. If he gets his hands caught in a net, that is the best way for him to get to it. The same goes for emerging from a torpedo barrel into the water. Combat swimmers lie in pairs inside the barrels, turned to face one another. In an emergency situation—e.g., loss of breathing apparatus—they both should be able to help one another. A large knife that can only be worn on the lower leg, would be wholly unsuitable because of the narrowness of the barrel. Therefore, most armed divers argue for knives with a small handle and not too long of a blade.

There is even a clearly defined profile for the sheath. It should be made out of a sturdy, seawater-proof synthetic material and have many attachment elements to enable the above-described carrying methods. For obvious reasons, the blade should not rattle around in the sheath or make other noises when the knife is pulled out of it. A hole in the bottom of the sheath allows water and dirt to flow out. The old tried-and-true rubber ring over the end of the handle is still the best solution for securing the knife in the sheath. However, most important of all innovations is corrosion protection, because officers and military personnel are encouraged to use their equipment as long as possible.

The use of totally rustproof or only very slowly corroding blade materials was not possible until the technical developments of the 1990s. This includes titanium, which is not at all affected by fresh or salt water. Titanium on the top surfaces provides a layer of oxide that permits no corrosion. Further advantages of this material are that it is 40 percent lighter than steel and completely antimagnetic. For minelayers and explosive removers (so-called Explosive Ordinance Disposal, or "EOD specialists"), this is a decisive, even life-saving advantage, because many ocean mines are equipped with magnetic fuses. Since pure titanium is too soft a material for blades, however, manufacturers turn to titanium alloys. The American company Mission Knives uses, for example, blades made out of a beta-titanium alloy with a hardness of 47 HRc. Under the Rockwell hardness scale this is a good hardness that knifemakers normally strive for with steel blades, but the titanium structure is more sound and the tendency for it to rub off is correspondingly lower. To be sure, the blades become dull more quickly. Because divers don't work

■ **Diver's knives with titanium blades are not only appropriate for Marines, but also for mine divers. From top: the "Oceanic," "MPT," "MPU" and "MPK" models, all from Mission Knives. Below, the "SK-T" from Seaman Subs.**

constantly with their knives under water, a well-sharpened knife can be used for a relatively long time, so long as there is no rust on the titanium sheath. Because of the high cost of raw materials for titanium and the special manufacturing costs, Mission Knives products are extra-ordinarily high-priced. In the area of titanium tactical diving knives, Mission Knives is still the undisputed market leader, although there are also less well-known manufacturers of titanium knives whose models have value in tactical use.

Of course, steel blades can also be appropriate for underwater use. Sea divers should make sure, however, that after every dive the knives be cleaned immediately with fresh water. One of the possible ways to protect steel blades against corrosion is to seal them with a coating of powdered epoxy, Teflon or Kalgard, which offers a high level of protection. To be sure, only unused blades are really protected; cut or scratched places on the coating are weak points from then on. After every use they have to be cleaned and water-proofed again.

The American Harold Carson is one of the few knife makers who manufacture tactical diver's knives. His model "U-2," which he designed together with an instructor from the U.S. military, contains a blade made of 440-C steel. This steel has a great cutting ability, but begins to rust quickly in salt water. To protect the blade from this hazard, Carson coated all the metal parts with olive-green Kalgard. Buck produces the commercial version of this knife in two models under the name "Intrepid," but in a pearlescent model without a Kalgard coat. Lately, Carson also has been designing his "U-2" with blades made out of talonite, a stainless alloy with a cobalt base.

The Solingen company Böker has adopted an extremely rustproof blade steel for its tactical maritime knife from the French firm Aubert & Duval. By applying nitrogen and using a special hardening method, the French achieve nearly total rust resistance for their X-15 T.N. steel. In addition, X-15 T.N. also offers the needed cutting ability. This material easily has the cutting ability of ATS-34 and 440-C. If it were antimagnetic to boot, it could also be used by minelayersminelayers could also use it. For general underwater use, this steel is one of the best by today's standards of technology, followed by titanium.

Maritime knives with so-called austenitic AISI 303 blades have only limited value. This type of steel cannot be hardened because of its low amount of oxygen. Used by and large in the area of food technology, it is, however, enormously rustproof precisely because of the lack of oxygen. Unfortunately, a non-hardenable blade has only limited value for cutting.

A few years ago, the American company Wenoka, which specializes in knives with austenitic steel blades, introduced a tactical maritime knife with a black blade called "Commando."

Survival Knives

The survival knife combines a whole range of characteristics that make up a tactical knife. As described on page 36 , the survival knife had already found its way into military equipment in the early 1960s. Among knife experts, the Randall Made Knives model "18 Attack/Survival" is considered a classic of its type. As we all know, the survival knife experienced a massive upswing in popularity because of the film industry. Just shortly after the release of the movie, Jimmy Lile's *Rambo (First Blood)* design was copied by countless knifemakers and manufacturers. Some were strongly oriented toward the original; others simply tried to keep the basic characteristics of the knife and incorporate their own ideas. In addition, there came a range of rather curious developments from the U.S.A., Japan and Spain. Also, in Germany and Switzerland, manufacturers like the Solingen firm Schlieper and knifemakers like Wolf Borger and the knife manufacturer Klötzli were preoccupied with this. The fascination with survival knives did not last long, however; already by the late 1980s the trend was over. One of the few knifemakers who made his entrance into the knife business with his survival knife and whose basic model is, even today after

■ **Opposite page: Steel versions, from top: "Commando" (Wenoka), "Orca" prototype (Böker), "Tiburon" (Buck), "Intrepid" (Buck), and the diver's knife "Barracuda" (Barakiri), which is officially supplied to German armed divers.**

Team 3 in Peril: Survival Story of a German Combat Diver

By Rüdiger Gaza

Storm winds whip the cold Baltic Sea: January, a moonless night, drizzling rain, almost completely clouded over, the water temperature at 2 degrees Celsius. Ideal combat diving weather and perfect for carrying out an underwater attack. Three combat diving teams (each team consisting of two divers tied together at the wrists by short ropes) prepare themselves for the underwater attack in the "Speedboat" (a special high-speed rubber dinghy). Goggles, rafts, underwater compasses, depth-measuring instruments, explosives, breathing apparatus and diver's knives. Each member is prepared, with just three more minutes until takeoff. The team leader gives his final orders. "Ready!" Team 1 gets on the prow of the "Speedboat" and jumps off at a speed of approximately 20 knots (ca. 37 km/hour). So do Teams 2 and 3. Finally, the boat takes off at high speed. From that point on, the six combat divers must depend on themselves and each other alone. "Now the hard part begins!" This means swimming to the diving site, about two sea miles (1 sea mile = 1,853 meters), and from there they will dive one sea mile down to reach their goal: a destroyer. The drill begins. The weather is improving: "Ready to dive." Equipment check. "Damn! Dirk lost his knife while swimming." Was this a loss of equipment an error in fastening it, or clumsiness? At this moment it makes no difference. The fact is, that Team 3 is missing a knife. "Hopefully it won't be needed later? Oh well! Knives are only ancillary equipment, kind of like driving gloves—just for decoration." They dive—the compass reading is 220 degrees. The teams are on their way. In about one hour they must all reach their goal. Then they must bring up the charge, return, get picked up by the "Speedboat" "at the rendezvous point, and return to home port. Zero hour—4:00: the boat waits to pick up the returning divers. 4:05: Team 1 is picked up and they make their report. Teams 2 and 3 should surface at any moment. 4:15: time is up, and the team leader is getting more and more nervous: Should he radio headquarters or wait? Decision: "Wait!" 4:30: The cold is gnawing at the diving team on the boat. S and still no signs of life from their four comrades. The team leader decides to inform headquarters and to send out the search and rescue team. Just at this moment, both teams surface next to the boat. What happened? After diving, Dirk and Bernd moved toward the object in the prescribed direction and at the tactically optimal depth. About 300 meters before their goal, Team 3 swam into a fishing net. Such nets are actually no problem for a knife, but Bernd was mercilessly trapped and Dirk could not free him because he had lost his knife. Minutes went by, even hours as it turned out. You could say it was lucky that both divers had been equipped with oxygen tanks for this drill. But even with this apparatus, the oxygen supply would eventually be exhausted. Just at that critical moment, out of the darkness two black shapes came swimming up to the unlucky duo—their comrades from Team 2. They assessed the situation immediately and with just a few cuts, their

The author, Lieutenant Commander Rüdiger Gaza, has over 28 years of combat diving experience in the German marines.

comrades were freed from the nearly fatal grip of the fishing net. The return was then child's play. During the subsequent debriefing in the barracks, the following sources of error were established in regards to the fishing net: Team 3's divers Dirk and Bernd had found themselves in a life-threatening situation. It was only through sheer luck and chance that Team 2 swam directly into them on the way back up. How could this serious situation have come about? Was the loss of the diving knife when entering the water due to attaching it incorrectly? How could such mistakes be avoided in the future?

1. Fundamentally, a diver's knife should be carried so that it can be reached with one hand and without contortions.

2. The ties should not be too old or breakable.

3. It should be neither too easy nor too difficult to pull the knife out of the sheath.

4. A diving knife should not be the size of a sword: "Smaller is better!"

Finally, it can be said that a diver's knife should be part of the equipment of every responsible diver. Just as with his other equipment, the diver's knife should be chosen on the basis of its handiness, quality, and carrying comfort, totally disregarding aesthetic criteria, and should be purchased according to these factors.

almost two decades, nearly unchanged, is South African Chris Reeve, who emigrated to the U.S. in the early 1990s. His knives are some of the most successful of their type.

A survival knife that is worth its price must possess a number of basic characteristics. In an emergency where it is the only tool available, its user should be able to accomplish all the tasks necessary to guarantee his survival in a hostile environment. In a military situation this means not only in nature, but also possibly also against enemy soldiers. A survival knife must take the place of a hammer, an ax and a shovel so that shelter can be built, and a saw to cut through wood, bone or metal. It should have a blade that is capable of slaughtering wild animals, and it should have a waterproof container that can hold matches, needles, pain medication and disinfectants. All of these requirements give the survival knife its typical characteristics. The blade should be between 15 and 20 centimeters long and be strong enough to lend the stability needed. Sharp dagger blades are completely inappropriate because these are not good for dressing or skinning animals. "Drop point," Bowie and "spear point" are the most prevalent blade shapes. In addition, serration on the rear third of the blade's edge increases its value.

The biggest cost in producing such knives is usually forming the sawteeth on the back of the blade, because these have to either be ground out or be cut in with a laser beam. Unfortunately, few manufacturers stand out in the way they make their

sawteeth; too often they only achieve an aggressive appearance. Before a knifemaker begins to construct and finish a serrated edge, he must be clear as to what is going to be sawed and whether the knife is going to be used for pushing or pulling. Saws made of different materials do not work equally well for the same task. So the form must be determined by the material to be cut. A wood saw should be able to cut freely. This means that it must run conically downward from the widest part of the saw so that it won't get stuck in the wood after just a few millimeters. On Lile's knives this is achieved with a wedge-shaped cut that extends over the entire breadth of the blade from the saw to the cutting edge. Knife manufacturers who are eager to copy Lile's design often misunderstand or simply overlook this detail. They merely give the same thickness to the serration on their knives, which makes the saw nearly unusable. A saw that runs conically toward the point can only cut through only a small strip and does not allow the rest of the blade's strength to be used. Anyone who tries sawing wood with such a knife will

■ The handy "Combat" survival knife from Lile Handmade Knives. On the sheath is an attachment for the sharpening steel.

eventually get stuck at the strongest part of the blade and will not be able to continue. Matters are different with softer materials like ropes, rubber hoses, etc., which fold open on both sides. Also, the length of the blade is a deciding factor on the success of the saw. The longer the blade (and therefore the saw), the fewer strokes are needed.

The surface of the blade should corresponding to the tactical requirements. While in civilian use the blades can be bright and reflective, in tactical use they should be matte and non-reflective. A polished blade is excellently suited for signaling.

A hollow handle is another typical feature of a survival knife. It must be watertight and offer enough room for certain important utensils, which, once again, depend on how the knife is to be used. Most first-generation survival knives had a compass on the end piece. But in most cases this proved inappropriate. The fluid-filled compass became loose over time, or the items in the handle tended to scratch and damage it. Hence, manufacturers like Buck and Chris Reeve have totally rejected the idea of putting a compass on the handle.

One weak spot in terms of survival knives has always been anchoring the blade onto the handle. The haft usually runs just a few centimeters into the handle and is secured from the outside by a peg that is either screwed or welded in on the inside and covered with an epoxy. If this is done professionally, the chance that the blade

■ Survival knives of the 1980s from Wolf Borger (above) and the knife manufacturer Klötzli. Both models are still made today for special orders.

Harald Moeller, a Canadian knifemaker of German descent, integrated a removable hand protector and a removal device for screwdriver jobs into his survival knife "Bearclaw II."

will become loosen is small. With his survival knives, knifemaker Chris Reeve invented a completely new method with a piece of circular steel. This solution eliminated the weak spot between the blade and the handle.

For the sheaths, most manufacturers chose leather, to which they added a pocket for a whetstone, or in the case of Lile, an "EZE-LAP" sharpening steel. In hindsight, leather was surely an adequate sheath material for the early 1980s. However, Buck paved the way from the beginning and designed a weatherproof, rugged synthetic sheath with a Cordura accessory pocket. On the back of the sheath there was also a sharpening surface for the cutting edge. One lot of these survival knives was given to the U.S. Navy SEALs to test, but they were not pleased with this heavy, complicated knife. The "BuckMaster Survival" knife stopped being produced in the late 1990s.

In contrast, Randall Made Knives, Lile Handmade Knives, Chris Reeve Knives and the knife manufacturer Klötzli still produce their survival knives in relatively unchanged form. This is certainly proof that quality endures.

Hatchet Knives and Field Knives

The term "hatchet knife" means a type of knife that can be used overwhelmingly as a tool but can also be used as a weapon. In the hands of a skilled fighter, it can have a terrifying effect because of the blade's size and weight. Just a look at one of these knives can be demoralizing. In the Falklands War of 1982, the British cleverly used propaganda pictures of Gurkha soldiers sharpening their traditional "Kurki" hatchet knives before an imminent attack. The result of the use of this propaganda, combined with far-reaching horrifying rumors, was that the Argentinians—who were mostly poorly trained, poorly equipped, drafted by their leaders and left to fend for themselves—were terrified when they first saw these weapons brandished by the Nepalese elite fighting forces. In contrast, similar propaganda connected with the "Smatchet" (see page 21), which likewise fell under the category of a hatchet knife, had far less of an effect on the Axis powers, even though some of the Commando soldiers pictured with their "Smatchets" could inspire fear in the beholder. But that was a long time ago.

Almost half a century later, in the early 1990s, a new trend brought the hatchet knife out of oblivion. They began to appear among the lines of civilian manufacturers as collector's knives and utilitarian knives, and soon new models were added. The American companies Cold Steel, Becker Knife & Tool and Ontario began offering these "Kukris." As opposed to the hand-forged Gurkha "Kukris" from Nepal, these blades were made from high-quality industrial carbon steel. Because they had to be extremely strong, they had a hardness of about 60 HRc. Unfortunately, carbon steel of this hardness is not rustproof. So Cold Steel and

■ The survival knife "Project I" from Chris Reeves Knives, which is extremely resilient because of its construction from a single piece of A-2 steel, has been on the market since the early 1980s.

Ontario covered the blades with a black powdered epoxy coating. Common among all three manufacturers is the use of synthetic handles, which ensure a firm grip. While Cold Steel's and Ontario's elastomer handles were directly sprayed on, Becker Knife & Tool molded polycarbonate handle shells onto the haft.

The "Smatchet" experienced a rebirth in the late 1980s because of Rex Applegate's involvement. At first only available as expensive, handmade individual pieces from the workshop of knifemaker Bill Harsey, the "Smatchet" later was made by Buck, Al Mar and the German manufacturer Böker. Harsey used L-6 steel for his

■ The Nepalese Gurkha has always had an excellent reputation as a fighter. This one is sharpening his "Kukri" with a typically small knife.

TACTICAL KNIVES

The official "Kukri" model of the Gurkhas is, then as now, ground by hand.

"Smatchet," which had a hardness of over 60 on the Rockwell scale. On the other hand, industrial manufacturers preferred to rely on stainless steel; Buck used 425-M, Al Mar A-6, and Böker 440-C. All three chose polycarbonate for the handle material. In addition, Al Mar and Böker offered models with Micarta handle shells.

The knives made by the American manufacturer Busse are more tools than weapons. Likewise made from carbon steel and available with either an elastomer handle or Micarta handle shells, the larger models definitely fall under the category of field knives in tactical use. Becker Knife & Tool's "Tactool" is purely a tool. It does not look very elegant, but it is useful for building shelters or opening doors or windows.

Below: Modern "Kukris" from Becker Knife & Tool ("Machax") and Cold Steel ("Mini Gurkha Light Kukri" and "Gurkha Kukri").

■ This should teach the Wehrmacht the meaning of fear: propaganda photo of a British Commando soldier with a "Smatchet."
Photo: Imperial War Museum/H17456

A truly exotic specimen among hatchet knives and field knives is the Chilean "Korvo" ("raven"), which gets its name from its hooked blade. This knife has a radically bent carbon steel blade that is reminiscent of a primitive tool for field work and whose design doubtless derives from that. Chilean elite and special forces are equipped with this knife, which serves as a weapon, tool, and elite insignia. The state-owned arms manufacturer FAMAE produces it with two different blade variants.

Concealed Knives

Wearing a knife concealed has two distinct tactical advantages: (1) The knife cannot be seen, and its wearer looks unarmed. (2) The wearer has the element of surprise on his side in case he has to use his knife—an advantage that is not to be taken lightly depending on the situation. The same criteria, of course, also apply to the use of folding knives. But many professional users in the field of security prefer a fixed-blade knife. The blade does not have to be opened first, which can prove to be a source of risk for accident and injury under extreme stress. The tactical advantage of taking less time to pull out the knife, as mentioned above, is probably not such an issue today now that modern one-handed knives and

■ The "Smatchet" was one of the favorite weapons of hand-to-hand combat specialists Fairbairn and Applegate. This photo shows a handmade one-of-a-kind piece from knife maker William Harsey (left) and Böker's series model.

■ Above: Big, heavy and black. From left, field knives from Busse Knives ("Combat Basic 7"), Colt ("Jungle Commander") and Becker Knife & Tool ("Brute" and "Magnum Camp").

■ Right: Because of the unusual shape of its blade, the "Tactool" from Becker Knife & Tool is a truly exotic specimen among tactical knives.

■ Symbol of the
Chilean elite forces:
the "Korvo" from
FAMAE.

switchblades can be opened with lightning speed.

With fixed-blade knives, size is a deciding factor. Of course, the total length should not exceed a certain point, otherwise not only is it less comfortable to carry, but it greatly hinders the anatomy when pulling it out. Fairbairn explained this problem as early as the 1930s, when he served as a police officer in Shanghai. Together with two of his friends, Samuel Yeaton and Sam Moore, both of whom were American Marines, he developed a concealed leather shoulder holster, which held the knife with the grip upside down. This method is, then as now, one of the most widely used ways of carrying a concealed weapon.

The first "concealed" knife did not appear on the knife market until decades later, if one does not consider all of the individual secret service weapons that were treated as collector's items. The "new" ones were called "boot knives." Generally equipped with a steel spring clip on the back of the sheath, it could be attached to the shaft of a boot, the waistband of a pair of trousers, or the inside breast pocket. Unfortunately, the clip was usually attached to the sheath in such a way that it only allowed the knife to be carried with the handle up. In the case of carrying it in the waistband that was fine, but it was wrong for the other two methods. If someone wanted to grab for his knife in his boot, he would first have to pull his pantslegpants leg up over his boot. It would have been more practical to attach the sheath with the handle upside down; that way, the user would only have to reach between his trousers and his boot. Similarly, the breast pocket carrying method was flawed. Here, the arm would have to bent bend in an angle in front of the chest, and the knife would be pulled out in a half-circular motion with the blade passing in front of the face. From a tactical standpoint, the boot knife wearer would lose the element of surprise, and the person carrying his knife in his inside breast pocket would end up injuring himself.

Among the first well-known boot knives are Gerber's "Mark I" and "Command I," as well as Kershaw's "Trooper." For the second generation of its model "Guardian," Gerber further developed its sheath system so that it allowed much more variation in carrying methods.

In the early 1980s, knifemaker Tom Maringer gained attention with his concealed sheath system made out of Kydex. His colleague Bud Nealy improved upon this idea

■ **Columbia River Knife & Tool issues its "Polkowski/Kaspar" model standard with two sheaths, which allows it to be carried concealed.**

by developing a whole assortment of Kydex attachment devices. To be as least conspicuous under clothing as possible, Nealy's knives are very flat. Originally only available with Tanto blades, today his collection contains a number of blade shapes. In 1998 he transferred the licensing rights for his sheath system to Böker, which produces a slightly different version of his knife with various blades and handles. Besides Böker, Columbia River Knife & Tool produces a comparable carrying system, although with polyamide sheaths.

■ **The MCS carrying system ("Multi Concealment Sheath") from Bud Nealy allows can easily be attached to various parts of the body. The knife pictured here is a "Specialist" model from Böker.**

■ Almost too pretty to carry: the "Persian Fighter" with the extravagantly made "Execulite" shoulder carrying system from knifemaker James Piorek.

One of the stars among knifemakers who make concealed knives is James Piorek. He offers a strongly Japanese-inspired knife along with a comprehensive range of carrying systems, which can be attached under the upper arm, on the back or on the underarm. In particular, his shoulder carrying system "Execulite" makes it possible to comfortably carry and pull out knives with rather long blades.

Other trendsetters are those knives that can be easily carried around the neck in a Kydex sheath on a chain or nylon cord. Thus, in American jargon they are called "neck knives." So that they do not fall off, it is recommended that they be carried under a sweater or T-shirt. Neck knives can be carried relatively easily and comfortably, as long as they are not too heavy or large. For this reason, knifemaker knifemaker Walter Brend makes his knives in a skeleton form or with very flat Micarta handle shells. Bud Nealy favors chains over nylon ropes. According to his estimation, a nylon rope presents a potential danger for the wearer if matters take a turn for the worse and the enemy is able to grab on to the rope. In contrast, the chain rips off at a particular pressure point. That way, strangulation is not possible.

■ The "Execulite" shoulder carrying system from James Piorek guarantees lightning-quick access (shown here unconcealed for better perspective).

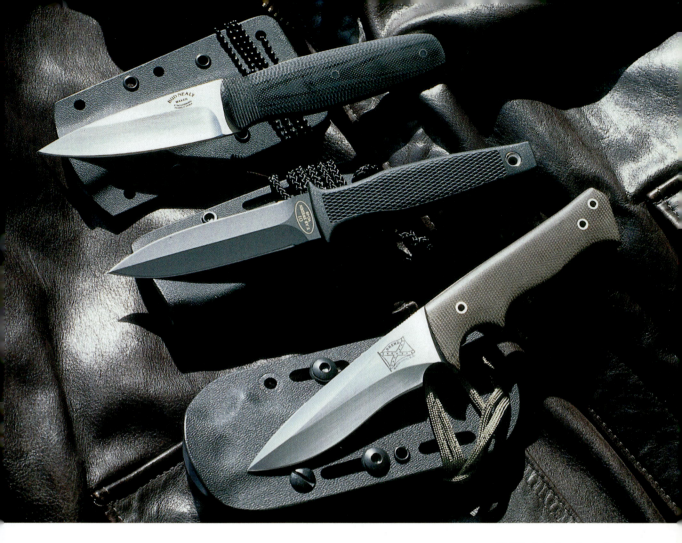

■ "Neck knives" can be carried comfortably on a rope or chain around the neck. From top: The "Kinzhal" model from Bud Nealy, the "Garm" from Fällkniven, and Walter Brend's neck knife.

Tactical Knives With Special or Auxiliary Functions

Because virtually every type of knife for tactical use has been introduced in the foregoing chapters, this section will examine knives with only one specialized function or with interesting auxiliary functions. No distinction will be made between fixed-blade knives and folding knives, insofar as they serve the same purpose.

Cutting knives

Perhaps the most exotic, and at the same time the most underestimated, knife design is that of the cutting knife. While many contemporaries imagine this instrument to be a particularly cruel and brutal combat knife, it is actually less appropriate for this purpose in the classic sense. Precise stab wounds cannot be accomplished with it, and neat cutting is also not possible. The sickle-shaped blade, in American jargon called

■ **Rescue knives are excellently suited for cutting through belts. From top: models from Hubertus ("Rescue Tool"), Camillus ("CUDA-EMT") and Eickhorn ("RM-1").**

"Hawkbill," is best suited to cutting through ropes and straps. The blade looks somewhat like a claw, with which one can grasp a particular object and cut it up. Often only one hand is sufficient, without having to hold the object with the other hand. This is especially advantageous in situations where the user has only one hand free, while the other possibly holds a weapon for self-defense.

The first special forces outfitted with this kind of knife were the British Special Air Service ("SAS"). Although this knife was actually developed as an emergency rescue knife for pilots, the Aircrew Emergency Knife ("AEK") from Joseph Rodgers & Sons has belonged to the arsenal of this commando and anti-terrorism unit since the 1980s. During the attack on the Iranian embassy in London in 1980, the necessity for such a knife became very clear when an SAS officer was nearly trapped while rappelling and could have helplessly succumbed to the flames in the burning building if not for some quick cutting action with an "AEK."

As an alternative to the British "AEK," the U.S. company Columbia River Knife & Tool offers its "Bear Claw" model, which likewise has a fixed sickle blade.

In the area of folding knives with rescue blades, there are far more models and manufacturers, including Camillus, Columbia River Knife & Tool and Spyderco. Besides the sickle blade, there is also the hook blade, which can be found on the

■ **The AEK from Joseph Rodgers & Sons saved the life of an SAS man during the attack on the Iranian embassy in London in 1980.**

The background picture comes from the book *SAS im Einsatz* by Peter Macdonald, published by Motorbuch Verlag in 1994.

Using Knives During Parachute Jumps:
The Experience of a Bundeswehr Paratrooper

It's 22:00 local time, at the Nochten the training area near the German-Polish border. *Luftwaffe* transport airplanes, Transall C 160C-160s, rumble over the extensive forested area of the Moscow heath. On board each plane are 60 paratroopers of the airborne brigade of the German army. The paratroopers are to be dropped in three waves for each of the three planes during a night jump onto the practice site—not an everyday task during *Bundeswehr* drills, and certainly not without risk at night.

It is very dark at this time of night and in this area—substantially darker than many other areas of the country, which are more densely populated and are consequently more brightly lit up at night. The pilots are highly focused; the orders for the final approach of the *Einsatzleitgruppe* (Lead Mission Group, "ELG") are to move the paratroopers toward the ground using the right flight maneuver. The direction of approach, altitude, wind direction and speed—everything must be perfect. The camouflaged troops of the airborne brigade's advance party, who are deployed on the ground, listen to the sounds of the motor and strain to peer into the darkness. Despite the darkness, it seems to the soldiers on the ground that the "country yardstick" of the tank runway is invisible to mark the landing site. The ELG has given the green light, and the jump can begin.

At 300 meters high, the world looks different. The nighttime landing site in the open fields, rising up so clearly against the surrounding forest scenery, is only an indistinct spot of light on the carpet of land, which seems to be engulfed in shadows beneath the aircraft. Just one tiny drift in the approach toward the lead marking on the ground, barely glimmering in the night, would bring—together with unlucky winds— serious problems to the paratroopers, who are equipped with round parachutes that are difficult to control.

The side doors in the Transall are opened, and the first paratroopers stand ready to jump out. In the plane outside to the left, a field officer is at starboard and a sergeant major is at port. Orders for assemblage on the ground are clear, and both of them await the sound from the P.A. over their heads and the "Go!" from the person who will push them out. Honk—green light—the paratroopers exit the planes in rapid succession. Chin to chest, legs crossed and hands on their reserve parachute—at night and with a full pack everyone pays close attention to the proper jumping procedure and counts precisely: "Hupp—one thousand—two thousand—three thousand—four thousand!" Their chutes open with a swoosh, and silence enfolds them. The sergeant major at the port door looks around. As far as he can tell, the irregular double row of open chutes is floating behind him through the night sky. The field officer who jumped with him at the same time is already floating further down because of his greater body weight and more equipment. Just as the experienced NCO moves to release the parachute pack, the crashing and crunching of branches reaches his ears. The bigger, heavier paratrooper sweeps through the treetops of a thick forest brush. Something has gone wrong: The paratroopers landed diagonal to the planned approach because of a strong ground wind on the edge of the jump site. The first two encounter an old stock of trees, which towers over the open field like a peninsula, and the rest fall into a forest plantation area behind it. As the breaking and scraping of branches and twigs around the sergeant major ceases, the reason is apparent: his sideways roll during the fall was halted by the straps and catchlines of his parachute and the outlet line on his parachute pack. Cursing under his breath, he loosens the buckles on his straps, rips the harness and reserve parachute from his body and pulls his backpack toward him. He is bruised all over. Not far away, there is another crashing sound in the woods. About 30 meters away, the officer finds his sergeant major several meters up, wedged tightly in the branches of a tree. "Taking a break up there?" comes up the offhanded question up from the forest floor. "Not really, Lieutenant Colonel, but I'm hanging all tangled up here at seven thirty!" Indeed, landing in the tree put the paratrooper in an unfortunate situation. He was not only hanging in the branches, but he had also caught himself in the catchlines of his parachute and those of the reserve parachute that had opened as he was scrambling around, as well as in the outlet line of the pack.

"I'll get out! We don't need security, Lieutenant Colonel!" The sergeant major assesses his situation in a no-nonsense manner. "I'll just cut myself out!" "Good, Tarzan, I'll come up and help you!" This situation is just too ridiculous, think both men. Of all places, both of us old hares land in the trees. Gossip for the whole battalion...

In this situation an old piece of paratrooper's equipment, often smiled at by outsiders, proves worthwhile: the parachute-cutting knife. More compact than a large combat or survival knife and always worn on the same place of the body (typically in a pocket on the right thigh and not on the "disposable" uniform), the soldier intuitively finds it in an emergency, and, thanks to its construction and function, opens it with one hand and uses it right away. In the final analysis, it doesn't matter whether the blade "falls" or is spun out of the handle as with traditional German fall knives or cutting knives, or whether it's one of those contemporary one-hand designs. The important things are its accessibility, its sharpness, whether it (preferably) has sawteeth for ripping and cutting, a secure and reasonably comfortable handle and a rugged blade. Of course, the knife should also be able to take care of everyday jobs without wearing out too fast, and, if necessary, be used in hand-to-hand combat as the *ultima ratio*. Its main function, however, is obvious at this tree landing.

The sergeant major has pulled his knife and made a few cuts to free himself from the tangled catchlines. Then he loses his hold, has to suddenly stabilize himself and grabs on with both hands. In doing so, the opened knife slips and falls. "Is that supposed to be an attack?" asks the lieutenant colonel climbing the tree, as the knife comes whistling right in front of his nose. That's right—why is a catchline or something similar supposed to be tied to the pommel? Because that way the knife can be secured to the man during the job, which possibly might have to be involuntarily interrupted, and it won't disappear—in the worst case scenario, never to be seen again—into some abyss!

With their combined strength and the battalioner's cutting knife—incidentally, not a service-issued folding knife—the sergeant major, together with his equipment, is cut free in a matter of minutes. A true "tactical" reaction avoiding noise, artificial light and increased movements on the landing site, which during a real mission can happen only too often on the battlefield, insofar as putatively securely hidden air landings can be discovered by the enemy. To be sure, this requires caution and prudence, also during practice and training sessions during peacetime. Many paratroopers have severely injured themselves by falling out of the treetops after landing if suddenly the "supporting parts" break away! Therefore, commanders must be alerted of such practice plans beforehand, in order to rescue paratroopers from trees. But that is another story.

This imaginary and real experience makes the usefulness and importance of a knife for the military paratrooper obvious. Consistently carrying a concealed multifunction knife represents without doubt a very important field-worthy piece of equipment. That's exactly why the paratrooper has developed a special relationship to it.

■ The necessity of carrying cutting knives during a jump was conveyed to the author during a practice jump with paratroopers and marines.

so-called "rescue knives." Its job consists solely of cutting through ropes and straps without injuring the rescuer. Generally there is also a short cutting blade behind the hook, mostly serrated, with which narrow ropes can be cut through. Rescue knives are offered by, among others, the German companies Hubertus and Eickhorn.

A combination weapon/rescue knife is the Masters of Defense model "CQD." The main blade is formed in a spear point for tactical use, while on the end of the handle two additional support blades are stored, which are designed for cutting straps.

Glassbreakers

Besides cutting ropes and straps, breaking (car) windows is one of the most common tactical scenarios. Modern window glass is extremely shatterproof. For smashing glass, a striking instrument with the smallest point possible, in which force is concentrated, is necessary. Everyone at one point has seen the little red emergency hammers with ball peens, which in most passenger busses are located next to the windows. The idea to integrate these small yet efficacious ball points as an auxiliary function on a knife is natural.

A whole range of companies, including Masters of Defense, Meyerco and Eickhorn, have adopted this idea and outfitted special models with glassbreakers made out of carbide or tungsten. Knifemaker Stefan Steigerwald realized the same idea with a titanium ball on his tactical integral knife.

■ **Above: A titanium glassbreaker is located on the pommel of Stefan Steigerwald's fully integrated tactical knife.**

Training Knives

Safe handling of a knife, whether used offensively or defensively, is learned only through practice. However, to reduce the risk of injury, knives with sharp blades

should not be used for this purpose; rather, so-called training knives are used. These come in many varied models, either as knives made of artificial material or as regular knives, but with a dull blade. For knives made of artificial material, rubber is used, as for the Böker "A-F Training Knife," or extremely hard synthetic material, such as are produced by the companies Blue Gun or ASP. With the Böker model, the cutting edges are flat and can be prepared for marking the target with chalk or lipstick. A disadvantage is that it is very light in comparison to the original model. In this respect, versions made of hard synthetic material are a little closer to the real thing.

In the folding knife segment of the market, Spyderco and Benchmade offer a range of training knives of their well-known models. With these they replaced the qualitatively high-value blades with some of lesser steel quality and with strongly rounded-off points in order to avoid injuries. Using these models, quickly and safely opening and closing the blade can be practiced without danger. The greatest advantage, however, is their weight, because they can barely be distinguished from their "sharp" counterparts and, therefore, allow for realistic practice. Of

fundamental importance is that users must make sure to wear safety goggles during training. Getting struck in the eyes, even with a dull blade, can have fatal tragic consequences.

Knife-Firearm Combinations

Combining firearms with knives is not new. Many people over the centuries have tinkered with this idea with varying success. Most

■ Knife-firearm "Hybrid" from Global Research and Development.
Photo: G.R.A.D.

modern knife-firearm instruments fire from one to three shots, for example the "Triple-X" from the Swiss company Blitz-Mechanik. With this model, the user must decide, depending on the situation, whether to put the blade or the firing mechanism on the handle. Both of these cannot function at the same time. The latest version of a knife-firearm combination is the "Hybrid" model from Global Research and Development (GRAD). The barrel, which is integrated into the handle, holds five .22 caliber cartridges. Like a revolver, a trigger-like device located on the bottom of the handle releases the round and turns the barrel. This weapon can only logically be used at close range, because there is no way to aim it, and the efficacy of the .22 caliber bullet is limited. Thus, from a tactical standpoint, this knife is only practical

■ Left: Training knives allow for practice without injury. Pictured here are Spyderco's folding models with dull blades and red handles, as well as the fixed-blade "A-F" synthetic knife from Böker.

if one is prepared to use the knife and suddenly finds himself facing more than one enemy. The possibility of firing several shots is an important tactical advantage. Of course, firing a shot also attracts undesirable attention because of the loud bang. GRAD offers the "Hybrid" model as a tactical knife as well as in a bayonet version for the American M-16/AR-15 assault rifle.

Ballistic Knives
Besides the knife-firearm combination, there is also the possibility of firing the blade itself. One of the few well-known models that has been produced in fairly large numbers originated in the Soviet Union in the 1980s. It was supplied to the KGB and the special forces *Speznaz*. The functional principle is based on a blade being pressed and locked into place by a strong spring in the hollow handle. Similar to a hand grenade, a peg ensures that the trigger will not be released unintentionally. After this peg is pulled, one merely has to move one of the two-sided mounted security bolts, and the blade shoots out. The effectiveness of such a weapon and its possibilities for tactical use are certainly rather questionable.

■ Ballistic knives produced by Ostblock. The blade is fired by means of a spring.
Photo: VS-BOOKS Schulze & Verhülsdonk GbR

TACTICAL KNIVES

Throwing Knives

Who is not familiar with those scenes from Hollywood westerns, action movies and war films, in which the enemy is put out of action by means of a well-aimed throwing knife? The reality is considerably more sobering. To attain any kind of statistical accuracy with a throwing knife requires intensive training. The rotation of the blade and the distance of the target play a decisive role. However, a direct hit is never guaranteed. The author has noted during throwing demonstrations by well-known experts that even these specialists make errors over and over again. During a possible combat scenario, where an enemy needs to be taken out of commission at an unknown distance by means of a throwing knife, success is very doubtful. If the enemy moves or if he's wearing a ballistic safety vest, the chances are even worse. If the knife is misthrown, the thrower is discovered, and worse yet, the same knife can now be used against him. Rex Applegate once told the author that knife throwing belongs in the circus and not on the battlefield. Nevertheless, there are a number of throwing knives and axes on the market whose construction makes them suitable for tactical use. A good example is the "Viper I" model from knifemaker Harald Moeller, which can be used, above and beyond pure knife throwing, as a tactical knife as well.

■ The German-Canadian knifemaker Harald Moeller makes the best throwing knives in the world. This photograph shows his "Viper I" model in the modified "Tactical" design.

The Handle: Design Aspects and Materials

To carry and use a knife properly, it is important that the handle fit the anatomy of the hand in an optimal fashion. A good example of the development of a handle according to tactical and anatomical standpoints is the knife designed by Applegate and Fairbairn. In Applegate's opinion, a blindfolded soldier given a number of knife handles to grasp would always choose that of the "A-F" knife because of its good grip. No doubt Applegate was right, but he had had that opinion for decades. The "A-F" knife does indeed have one of the best handles, but other knife makers and manufacturers have also been incorporating similar considerations into their designs for years.

Many factors influence handle design, but the most important criterion is protecting the hand from the blade. A knife is of no use whatsoever if the user has to pay attention to his fingers while performing a task. Therefore, it must be ensured that the handle, independent of the grip or the tactical maneuver of the user, sits fits firmly in the hand. This requirement goes for folding knives as well as for knives with fixed blades. Other than prominent hand protectors, other very important innovations have emerged such as ramp-shaped thumb supports and diagonal

■ With his "A-F" knives, Rex Applegate succeeded in designing an ideal shape for the handle, which corresponded to the anatomy of the hand.

combs in the area of the thumb and index finger, which increase resistance to motion and thereby ensure safety. Bob Terzuola was one of the first knife makers to include these functional elements in his knife designs.

Improvements and innovations have been applied not only to the forms of handles, but also to the materials. Natural materials like wood, horn or leather are rare on modern tactical knives, which are intended for rugged use, because such materials are only marginally resistant to the elements. Synthetic materials, which are extremely rugged and resilient, have become much more common. Resilience is an absolute requirement

■ **The design and material determine the functionality of a handle. From left: aluminum (Spyderco's "Ayoob"), steel (Spyderco's "Police"), polyamide (Columbia River Knife & Tool's "Kaspar"), and G-10 (Böker's "Brend").**

for a knife whose handle might be used to break through a window pane or for other similar jobs. The predominant handle colors are black and olive green. Metals like titanium, aluminum and steel likewise have a solid place as handle materials in the field of modern tactical knives, but mostly on folding knives. Because it is becoming increasingly difficult to stand out from the competition with the plethora of tactical knives available on the market, many manufacturers are constantly trying to find new materials to market. These materials should only be considered established materials in a limited capacity, if at all, but the new material specifications do point to different, more modern and even better materials.

To form a more easily understandable and comparable picture of the flood of materials and material specifications, the following chapter presents the materials (and, to an extent, the way that they are produced) that currently exist on the market.

Forms

In the practical use of a knife as a tool or weapon, the user changes his grip on the handle according to the situation. Someone who has to chop or cut through hard materials with a great expenditure of force clearly holds a knife differently than if he is delivering a precise stab in self-defense or performing a different tactical maneuver. Most manufacturers of tactical knives, therefore, take care to form the handle so that it offers the most possible ways of holding it, and they consider the anatomy of the hand to the greatest extent possible.

To better understand the form of a handle, it must first be explained how a knife should actually be held. There are four basic holds in the tactical field: the hammer grip, the icepick grip, the fencing grip and the reverse grip.

The hammer and icepick grips are natural ways of holding a handle. They are relied on by the user in daily activities that have the knife functioning as a tool around the house, on the job or in hobbies. The nature of these grips is very different than with the fencing and reverse grips, which stem from knife fighting and serve to extend the domain of the blade or to carry out the most effective maneuver possible. Fairbairn and Applegate were strong advocates of these tactical handle holds as early as WWII. In their books on hand-to-hand combat training, *Get Tough* and *Kill or Get Killed*, they gave precise instructions for such holds. The handle of the "A-F" knife is the precise incarnation of this philosophy.

In the fencing hold, the handle of the knife lies diagonally in the hand, while the thumb touches the top side of the handle. It can either increase the cutting power of the front portion of the blade or, supported against a hand protector which is bent forward, i.e., a ramp-shaped thumb support, it can direct the blade's thrust. The handle becomes voluminous in the middle in order to fill and secure the hand well. In the back, the blade once again becomes narrower so that it can be encased well by the little finger. Because there is a double-edged dagger blade on an "A-F" knife, the handle hold plays no role, since there is a cutting edge on both sides. It is a different matter with single-bladed knives. Here, it is important when first grabbing the knife to hold it correctly in the hand with the cutting edge down. With the introduction of the ramp-shaped thumb support in the early 1990s, a better fencing grip was developed for single-edged knives. Here, the thumb no longer lays parallel to the index finger, but farther forward. The effect strived for is the exertion of even more control and power on the front part of the blade. Typical examples can be found with Timberland's "Specwar" and "Aviator" models, the Buck "Nighthawk" or the "MPT" from Mission Knives.

■ The handle design of the Piorek model "Persian Fighter" allows for all kinds of grips, even including the reverse grip shown here.

Handle ridges support a secure grip on the knife during pulling motions. It should be noted that more than one ridge in the area of the index finger sharply decreases the possibility of different holds. If, for example, one wants to drive the knife with the cutting edge up, the sides of the ridges press uncomfortably into the palm of the hand. Also, it is extremely difficult to define an average ridge radius for different hand and finger sizes. Ridges that are either too large or too narrow make a knife uncomfortable to handle. If the fundamental decision is made to have only one grip position, and the hand fits well around the ridges, such a handle is ideal for rough cutting jobs. The "Model 14 Attack," developed by Randall for the U.S. Marines, is one of the first examples of this type of handle, and it is still made the same way today.

With hacking knives that are driven and stopped with relatively great force, a secure hold plays a decisive role. The pommel anchors the handle in the hand. Well-adapted to form and functionality are, for example, the handles of the Cold Steel "Kukri" models, the Böker "Smatchet," the Colt "Special Ops Machete," and the Busse "Battle Mistress."

The possible handle forms for knives with fixed blades are generally more numerous than those for folding knives, which also have to take into account the form of the blade in closed position. In addition, there is the gap for the blade safety, which, for reasons of functionality, simply must be located in a certain position. However, modern knife manufacturers' designs allow all known holds to be performed with a folding knife handle. Models like the "SOCOM" from Micro Tech, the "Stryker" from Benchmade and the "Hornet" from Masters of Defense can easily be held in the fencing hold and the reverse hold. The same goes for Gerber's folding knife "A-F," an almost identical copy of the fixed-blade version, complete with double-edged blade.

The handle form should always conform to the knife's function. With tactical knives that are made for non-specific uses, the handle should take into account natural holds as well as knife-fight holds. This is different than with handles that have a specific use profile, such as a machete, for example. Here, a fencing grip would rarely be used.

A general requirement for both types of knives is a hole on the tip of the handle to fasten a catch line. Even here, opinions differ as to whether this is absolutely necessary or not. In any case, however, manufacturers should offer the purchaser the option to make this decision for himself.

Handle Materials

Handle materials can be divided into two main categories, synthetic materials and metals. Besides describing the individual materials, the following sections also discuss how they are processed in the scope of knife manufacturing.

Synthetic Materials

What are the differences between the fiberglass-enhanced Zytel, Kraton, G-10 and Micarta, and what accounts for the price differences among the completed knives? Besides the cost of raw materials, which are often quite variable, it is often production, which results in the heavy use of machinery and intensive wear and tear on tools, that drives up the price. Synthetic materials for handles found their use as early as WWII, in the form of phenol resin (PF) for combat knives. With phenol resin, the age of fully synthetic manmade materials essentially began. As early as the beginning of the 20th century, L. H. Baekeland was working on the condensation of phenol and aldehyde. Under the trade name Bakelite, the first fully synthetic manmade material gained world renown. The source materials phenol and formaldehyde, which were available in great quantities, enabled the simple production of large quantities. A typical example of a WWII knife with Bakelite handle shells is the hand-to-hand combat knife from Puma pictured on page 16.

Synthetic materials experienced a real upswing together with tactical knives. In the search for ever-newer, more-modern and more-resilient high-tech materials, knife manufacturers discovered a number of synthetic materials that were appropriate for use as handle shells. Even if most knife handles never have to withstand the forces that these materials protect against by their characteristics, for marketing reasons customers can be told that a handle can stop a .45 caliber bullet. How much sense that kind of statement makes the reader can determine for himself. Perhaps the most important advantage of synthetic materials as opposed to all other comparable materials is their lighter weight in relationship to their resilience. And it is just this characteristic which that makes synthetic materials—along with their cheap construction—so important to the knife industry.

 The Württemberg weapons maker Heckler & Koch makes the handles of their "SOCOM" pistols as well as their knife handles using a spray-on process.

Photo: Böker Baumwerk

Thermoplastic Synthetic Materials

Thermoplastic synthetic materials can be molded under the influence of heat. The knife industry usually uses them when handle forms already have been made by injection-molding machinery. After the synthetic material has cooled and hardened in the mold, it can be reshaped without changing the characteristics of the material by reheating it. The advantage of this process is that the form is always exactly the same, and it is inexpensive to make large quantities. Afterwards, whether separate handle parts still have to be assembled or the whole grip is sprayed directly onto the haft as the last step of the process, the ultimate effort of reworking the handle is spared. Coarse erosive structures in the injection mold make it unnecessary to additionally spray the handle with sand in order to give it a matte, non-reflective surface. But other surface structures can easily be integrated into the form and do not have to be painstakingly worked into the handle. If the handle is sprayed directly onto the haft, it likewise insulates the blade from electricity. Furthermore, the kind of synthetic material used determines its functions, such as its hardness. According to the product profile, one can choose a softer synthetic material that "sticks" better in the hand, or an extremely firm material with which one can beat or hammer if necessary. The disadvantages of the injection-molding process are that investment costs for tools are high, and there is no flexibility in production. Making an injection-molding machine costs an enormous amount of money, which can only be recouped by selling large quantities of a product. Depreciation is often a problem. Depending on the shape of the form, when the parts are cooled they sometimes sink in. And retouching is not easy. Once the injection-molding machine is set up, only very limited modifications can be made. If the need for modifications is great, more money will have to be spent to start all over again with a new machine. However, if everything works right and the pieces produced have a market, this method of production is marvelously effective and reasonable. The synthetic materials used can also be sprayed on in nearly every color, which again allows for great variety.

The most commonly used thermoplastic synthetic materials for knife handles are polyamide (PA), polycarbonate (PC) and acrylnitril-butadine-styrol (ABS). Developed by the American company DuPont in the 1930s, polyamide is one of the most ubiquitous synthetic materials around. Some of polyamide's main properties are its high mechanical strength and its resistance to heat, electricity, fire, and chemicals.

In 1957, independently of one another and almost at the same time, the American company General Electrics and the German company Bayer AG developed a way to produce polycarbonate. Like polyamide, polycarbonate is characterized by its surface hardness, high mechanical strength and resistance to heat. In addition, it is amazingly transparent.

ABS is a blend of resin and elastomer. The success of this synthetic material is due to its excellent strength, resilience and surface hardness. Like polycarbonate, ABS was developed in the 1950s.

During the course of production, these three synthetic materials differ in their melting points and the extent to which they shrink. Among the most common brands of polyamide used in manufacturing knives are Zytel from DuPont and Grilon from EMS. The leading brand of polycarbonate is Lexan from General Electrics. Mission Knives uses the brand name Hytrel, likewise from DuPont, a thermoplastic polyester elastomer. This material combines the most important features of very resilient elastomers and flexible materials: outstanding toughness and pliability, flexibility at low temperatures, and the ability to maintain these characteristics at high temperatures.

Through the addition fibers (0.1 to 0.5 mm long) made out of glass, Kevlar or carbon, the properties of the synthetic materials can be changed. The synthetic material retains its external shape and the matrix assumes the force introduced by the fibers, the pressure of the fiber support and the combined weight of the fiber bundles.

Duroplastic Synthetic Materials
Handle manufacturers who prefer to create their forms mechanically turn to duroplastic synthetic materials. Duroplastic synthetic materials undergo chemical

changes when they are put into their final shape. They are bound together into a spatial grid through a chemical integration reaction. Because the structure of the molecules is altered, this hardening is irreversible: once a duroplastic synthetic material is shaped, it cannot be changed. As with thermoplastic synthetic materials, here too there is a matrix in which fibers are embedded. For the production of fiber-strengthened synthetic materials, the industry uses in particular polyester, epoxy, phenol and acrylic resins for the matrix. Epoxy resins are used overwhelmingly in manufacturing knives. The most common fiber types are glass, carbon, or natural fiber materials like linen or paper.

Fiberglass—better known in the knife industry as G-10— has been an established component of duroplastic synthetic materials for years. High-quality, alkali-free E-glass is used first and foremost; its tensile strength is significantly greater than that of steel. Because of its lower density (2.5 g/cm^3) as opposed to steel (7.85 g/cm^3) and aluminum (2.7 g/cm^3), it has enormous resilience in relation to its weight. Moreover, fiberglass is not flammable and is therefore fireproof. Among the first knife makers who claim to have discovered G-10 as a handle material is the versatile Bob Terzuola. Benchmade and Spyderco followed in the mid-1990s. G-10 can be worked in two ways. As is usual with other covering

materials, the contours can simply be ground in and then polished, given a satin finish or sanded. By doing so, the fiberglass connections are broken and an interesting lamination effect results.

Those who desire a rough surface that is easy to grip must use fiberglass as a flat shell, made in the following manner. First, the plate material is ground to the desired thickness, and then it is taken out of the plate using a computerized grinding machine. Here it is already possible, with specially formed grinders, to give the corners a grip-friendly shape. After this step, the top part of the handle shells is sanded to change the shape of the softer epoxy resin inside. Now the fiberglass is an embossed structure and provides a surface that is easy to grip. However, after this step the G-10 shell is now totally gray from the sanding. To make it appear black again, the surface has to be oiled. G-10 also comes in colors other than black, such as brown, blue and red. Knifemaker Greg Lightfoot makes some of his tactical knives with blue G-10 handle shells.

Besides G-10, there is also G-11, which Mad Dog Knives uses for their "ATAK" series.

In addition to fiberglass, carbon fiber is also used in the area of fiber-strengthened synthetic materials. It consists of more than 90 percent carbon and is produced either from pitch or by carbonizing polyacrylic fiber. Carbon fiber is even less dense than fiberglass (1.6 to 2.0 g/cm^3), yet its weight-bearing capacity is very good. In the medical field, carbon fiber is used to make implants, because it is well-tolerated

Same design, but different materials and production processes: the handle on the left was made of Micarta using a mold; the handle on the right was made of a thermoplastic polycarbonate using a spray-on technique.

by the body, and it enjoys a reputation as having the best dynamic qualities of all materials. In the knife industry, carbon fiber is generally used for decoration. Even though this material is very resilient, it is its interesting laminated look that counts. Carbon fiber knife handles are not as slip-proof as handles made from G-10. Like G-10, carbon fiber can be made into a shell and then ground into shape. To be sure, the laminated effect is somewhat lost by doing so. Generally, the shells are simply cut out of a whole plate and then they are already ready to be assembled. In contrast to G-10, the shells do not have to be sanded and oiled. Grinding the extremely hard carbon fiber often causes much wear and tear on the tools, which makes the finishing costs as well as the costs of raw materials very expensive. Knifemaker Warren Thomas uses carbon fiber for his blades not only for its interesting look, but also because it provides functional support for the blade.

■ G-10 handles for the Böker-Nealy "Specialist," after being molded. They will be subsequently be sanded and oiled.

Photo: Bernd Schlemper/Andreas Jatridis

Among the oldest strengthening fibers in the family of duroplastic synthetic materials are paper and linen—better known under the name Micarta, a trademark of Paper International. Phenol resin is used for the matrix. Micarta certainly has the weakest tensile strength as compared to fiberglass and carbon fiber.

Nevertheless, it has great weight-bearing properties and has been used as a handle material on tactical knives for many years. Randall Made Knives' models Models 14 "Attack" and 15 "Airmen" (see page 36) are two of the first knives that were equipped with Micarta handles in the 1960s, during the Vietnam War. The advantage of using Micarta instead of leather handles at that time is obvious: Micarta is rugged and does not rot in a hot, humid jungle climate.

■ Walter Brend sanding the form for a Micarta handle. The deeper it is etched into during the sanding process, the more visually interesting it is later.

Linen Micarta looks most beautiful when it is ground. Then, the surface can be

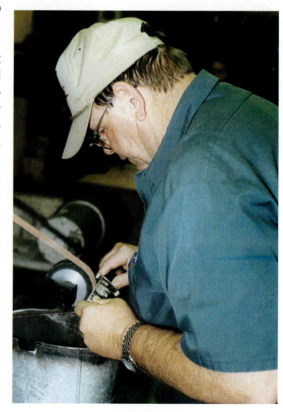

polished or sanded, which again markedly improves the grip and gives a matte finish to the handle. Micarta is available in a variety of colors. However, black, olive green and brown are mainly used for tactical knives.

Elastomers

On the other hand, those who want a softer, yet weight-bearing handle, like the ones Cold Steel made popular with their knives in the early 1980s, turn to elastomers. Their behavior is best compared to that of rubber: Elastomers are easily distorted, but like rubber, once the pressure is released, they go back to their original shape. Thus, elastomer handles are always somewhat sticky, a quality that is definitely desirable. Here, too, an injection molding process is used. Hardness and resistance to the elements depends on the various product types and formulas. Among the best-known brand names in the knife field are "Kraton" by Shell and "Santoprene" by Advanced Elastomer Systems.

Metals

Metals as handle materials are overwhelmingly found on folding knives. The reason for this is their high stability and precision. Of course, modern synthetic materials are extremely resilient, but they cannot do everything and they clearly have their limits. When knife manufacturers in the 1990s were just beginning to use G-10 to make handles, they still fixed screws into the shells. The same applied to the externally attached trouser clips. Because at that time manufacturers were still advertising

■ The "Terminator" dagger by Cold Steel is one of the forerunners of the 1980s elastomer handles.

with the claim that their knives could be taken apart to be cleaned, buyers naturally took the opportunity to do so. But after disassembling them several times, they discovered that the threads no longer worked. Even trouser clips, which were usually not unscrewed, would lock up due to the constant pressure on the screws. As a temporary solution, manufacturers began using screws with larger threads. But even here there is a point at which the knife cannot be repaired. Many manufacturers learned from these mistakes and screwed in steel or titanium detachment pieces on both sides. Unfortunately, there are only a few manufacturers who do this, as many did do not want to depart from the old method either because they do not know any better or because they do not want to do so because of the costs involved.

Another advantage of metal over synthetic materials lies in the how the blade is stored. If there is great crosswise pressure on the blade, embedding the blade storage in metal stops the handle shells from moving and possibly allowing the springs to be released and the blade to fold in. Handles that have to endure a lot of mechanical pressure are generally made out of metal. The best examples of this are modern switchblades whose handles are cut by computerized grinding machines. They are cut out of massive blocks of aluminum to a precision of hundredths of millimeters.

Three metals are commonly used in the area of tactical knives: steel, titanium and aluminum.

Steel

Steel was used as a handle material for tactical knives earlier than any other material. Spyderco provided the decisive impetus in the area of folding knives when it began making its knife models with high-quality stainless steel handle shells in the early 1980s. Knives that are made in Japan have shells made out of either AIA 410 or 420 steel, which is comparable to 1.4034 steel in Germany and likewise is used for blades. According to Glesser, steel shells simply offer the best stability for blade storage.

Although they have the advantage of being enormously stable, steel shells have their disadvantages, such as their great weight, their reflective surfaces, and their inadequate grip, all factors which that did not have the same importance in the early 1980s that they do today. Indeed, Spyderco later offered special tactical models with blackened handles and blades, but these were only available for a short time because Glesser was never completely happy satisfied with the different coatings.

In the area of fixed-blade tactical knives, steel handles are mostly found on survival knives. These are either fastened to the blade haft in a barrel shape or made out of one piece à la Chris Reeve.

(On the topic of steel, see also pages 150-154.)

Titanium

The use of titanium as handle material likewise dates back to the 1980s. At that time, Buck presented its first series of pocket knives with titanium handle shells. In the field of tactical knives, it was Bob Terzuola who gave this type of knife its stylistic appearance. Titanium is used primarily in aircraft and spacecraft technology, in chemistry (because of its great durability), and in medicine for implants. Among its properties are its great resilience, 40 percent lighter weight than steel, anti-magnetism, the fact that it is well-tolerated by the body, and its ability to change color through oxidation. Especially important, however, is its non-corrosiveness. At room temperature, titanium builds an oxide film on its surface that is constant, poreless and self-regenerating and that provides sustained protection against corrosion.

Among the most commonly used titanium alloys in the knife industry is 6AI-4V, which is known in Germany as 3.7165. This alloy, with proportions of about 6 percent aluminum (5.5–6.75) and 4 percent vanadium (3.5–4.5), and with a hardness of 5, is one of the most resilient titanium materials around. Especially important is the fact that 6AI-4V chips easily. This is a crucial requirement when grinding precision parts for handles, which will be functional later at computerized factories. Of course, in order to avoid expensive and time-consuming grinding processes, titanium can also be molded when cold, as Böker does. To be sure, this process requires extremely high pressure and the use of a titanium material with a hardness of 1. Since molded titanium has to fill the entire form, the material cannot be allowed to become fluid. For this reason a softer titanium alloy like of 3.7025 is chosen for this manufacturing method. All the other properties of titanium remain for the most part intact.

In the mid-1990s, knifemaker Chris Reeve developed his "Sebenza" model, which has a combination handle and locking system. With the "frame lock," the handle shells take on the function of a traditional spring according to the "liner lock" principle. To achieve durable, effortless functionality here as well, Reeve turned to the tried-and-true titanium 6AI-4V. This system is used with models from Columbia River Knife & Tool, Benchmade and Mission Knives, but under different names, of course. Combining a titanium interior with a G-10, Micarta or carbon fiber exterior is especially popular with tactical knives. To give titanium the mattest possible surface, it is usually sprayed with sand or finished with brushes and fine sanders (see pages 160–161).

The titanium shell of the "S-2" from Columbia River Knife & Tool also adopts the function of the blade lock ("frame lock").

Photo: Columbia River Knife & Tool

Aluminum

As early as the 1960s, Gerber developed a combat knife with an aluminum handle, the "Mark II." It is true that aluminum does not exhibit the hardness of steel or titanium, yet it does have some definite advantages over steel in the field. Like titanium, aluminum is very light, non-magnetic and resistant to corrosion. When exposed to air, a pure aluminum surface reacts with oxygen to create a thin but tight natural aluminum oxide seal, which protects it against further damage. Through ionized oxidation or "eloxidation" (electrolyzed oxidation of aluminum), the oxide coating can be strengthened and the aluminum surface can be made more corrosion-resistant. Moreover, it embellishes the metal and allows the surface to be painted in various colors. In the tactical field, it is usually a plain black or olive green, which is logical.

Aluminum handles are either made in a molding press or are ground, i.e., shaped, as a cast alloy from the pure material. Besides Gerber, Böker also uses a cast alloy for handle frames for its "Speedlock" model. To be able to use aluminum in a molding press, copper must be added to it. The disadvantage of cast alloys is that they are not easily eloxidized and that during pouring, small air bubbles, revealed by sanding, form just under the surface. Therefore, most aluminum parts are electroplated. For its "Speedlock," Böker chose a chrome coating that is not only decorative, but also protects the aluminum surface from scratches.

Many knife manufacturers also make their handle frames from an aluminum alloy with the American description 6061-T6. This is one of the many extremely hard

The Gerber models "Mark II," "Command I" and "Mark I" (from top) display classic examples of cast aluminum handles.

aluminum-magnesium-silicon alloys and it is very durable. Because there is no copper in it, it is very resilient in its unprotected state. It is also well suited for eloxidation and hard ionization. Hard ionization is a special variant of ionized oxidation. It results in a particularly thick, hard, damage-proof oxide coating.

There was a lot of grinding of aluminum cast alloys in the early 1990s because of the use of modern computerized factories. The precision and fit that can be achieved using this method of production are enormous. Companies like Benchmade and Micro Tech based their reputations on producing high-quality switchblades with aluminum handle shells. A disadvantage of computer-ground shells is the rather angular shape of the handle. Were a curved handle desired, the grinder would have to cut off interminable radius parameters, which would entail even more expense to run the machines.

Hilts, Pommels and Thumb Supports

Hilts and pommels protect the hand from the blade. They not only keep the fingers from unintentionally sliding onto the cutting edge(s), but also prevent the knife from getting dropped when pulling it out. From a tactical standpoint, the pommel has an additional function: in can be used for beating in hand-to-hand combat, and can also be used to break windowpanes. A good example is the pommel of Case Cutlery's "V-42 Stiletto," whose handle end was formed just for this purpose. Some manufacturers reject a special pommel and achieve the same effect with the haft, which they intentionally allow to project a few millimeters out of the end of the handle. Americans also talk of a "skull crusher."

Hand protectors on fixed-blade knives can either be assembled as separate parts, be constructed out of the whole material in an integrated fashion, be sprayed on with synthetic material, or be formed out of the haft itself. The latter is certainly the cheapest method, but it offers the least protective surface for the fingers. Of course, other standards apply for concealed knives, which reject wide hilts in order to be as "flat" as possible.

A chrome-nickel-steel alloy or brass are the classic materials used to make separately assembled hilts. The form of the hilt definitively decides which handle holds are possible. A cross-shaped hilt generally allows only natural grip variants, which certainly is not wrong for hatchet knives. But the cross-shaped hilt really gets in the way of a fencing grip, because the thumb presses uncomfortably against the vertically turned surface. A hilt that is turned slightly toward the front, à la Applegate-Fairbairn, is more comfortable and allows for the most possible tactical grips.

Of course, one can also do without the upper portion of the hilt altogether. But then the thumb should be given an additional support. Thumb supports can be either flat or slightly raised in order to give the middle finger a larger support surface area, and hence more resistance, when thrusting. So that the thumb won't change its position, most thumb supports are ridged to prevent slipping. This goes for fixed-blade knives as well as folding knives. In some cases these ridges can also be found on the end of the handle. These ensure a secure knife in the reverse grip.

On pocket knives, ridges plates are also used in the areas of the thumb and index finger. This is especially necessary if the shape of the handle does not offer any protection against the cutting edge. If the fingers slip onto the cutting

■ The hilt on the integrated knife "TAC 11" from Tom Johanning (left) is made of a single piece and only extends down on one side. For a better thumb grip, Johanning etched ridges into it. The two-sided steel hilt on the "A-F" knife (right) is bent forward to take the pressure off the thumbnail.

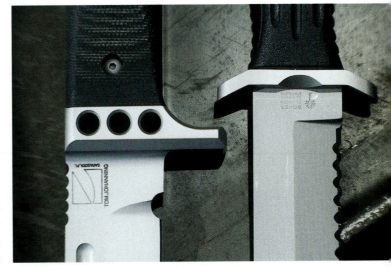

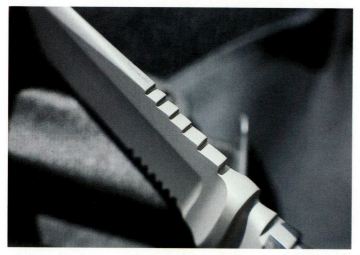

edge during a mission, the consequences could be fatal. To avoid accidents, the ridges should be well-placed according to anatomical and tactical considerations.

Another possible way to anchor the handle firmly in the hand during a pulling motion is to put the hilt between the index and middle fingers, insofar as the blade has a corresponding gap. However, this method presents the danger that the index finger will slip onto the cutting edge in the heat of battle and start be injured. To prevent this, some manufacturers add a second hilt. That way, the hand is protected in front by the main hilt, while the second hilt (sub hilt) stops it from slipping backward. American knifemaker Bob Loveless introduced this principle with his "Big Bear" knife. Of course, users of "sub hilt" knives are restricted to a single grip because the handle cannot be turned in the hand. For this reason, most "sub hilts" have blades with two cutting edges. The same goes for knuckle

■ **Above: A very different thumb support: Steigerwald cut an asymmetrical support into his tactical knife.**

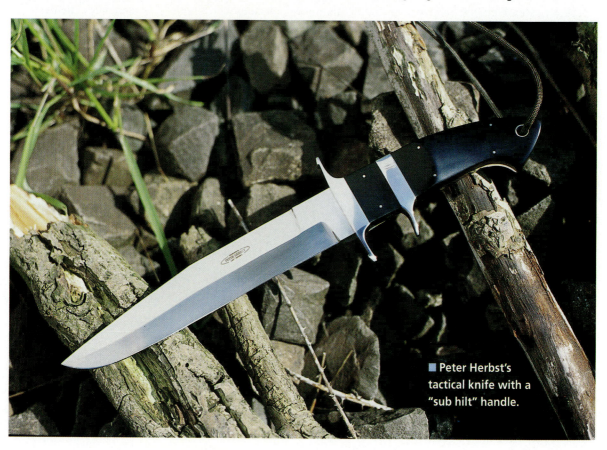

■ Peter Herbst's tactical knife with a "sub hilt" handle.

knives that have brass knuckle or D-ring-type side pieces to protect the fingers. However, the utility of knuckle knives, which are designed solely as weapons, is debatable. Besides, in many countries their use is legally restricted.

■ Knives with knuckle grips or D-rings are used more as weapons and less as tools. Here, Jack Crain's "Die Harder" model.

Blades and Their Importance in Tactical Deployment

Blades are certainly the most fundamental element to consider in relation to the tactical value of a knife. That the blade has to be sharp to fulfill its main function is just as much common sense as it is a limiting requirement, because only one sharp cutting edge also guarantees safe handling of a knife. If the blade is dull, the user tries to compensate by exerting more effort or using poorly controlled motions. It is easy for the tactical user to understand that this can have fatal consequences during a mission.

But how exactly should a blade be made? What is the right size, and how should it be shaped? These and other questions cannot be answered with one sweeping response. Every professional

■ **Blade forms and materials determine the use of tactical knives. From left, the Spyderco models "Chinook," "Starmate" and "Military" with CPM-T-440-V steel blades, as well as the "Sifu" (Round Eye Knife & Tool), made out of modified D-2 steel.**

user certainly has his own personal philosophy on this subject. As already discussed, the fact that the blade of a tactical knife should serve equally as knife and tool to the greatest possible extent is the main concept behind this type of knife. But because of the specific task that the knife has to fulfill in each individual case, it can happen that it can be used more as a weapon on one occasion and more as a tool on another occasion. Thus, every buyer should have a specific profile of which particular task(s) for which he is going to use his knife. A cutting knife with a sickle-shaped blade is rather unsuitable for use as a survival knife or diver's knife. The blade material also plays an important role. Which alloys are appropriate for diver's knives, for example? Anyone who does not want to be unpleasantly surprised on a mission should definitely take these and other considerations into account.

For a long time now, steel has not been the only blade material available. Modern materials like titanium, ceramic and synthetic materials have opened up a number of tactical possibilities that years ago would have been unimaginable.

Additional factors that determine the tactical utility of a blade are, for example, serration and dovetailing. Since Spyderco made serration popular in the early 1980s, tactical knives can no longer be imagined without it. Of course, there are very contrary views on this topic as to how the serration should look and on which side of the blade it should appear. To avoid bringing attention to the blade by reflecting light, the surfaces of tactical knife blades are treated. The following sections describe what possibilities exist for this and the value of each individual process.

This book consciously omits the topic of damascus steel, because it plays no role in the area of tactical knives, as opposed to collector's knives. The reader is directed to the general technical literature for more on that subject.

Shapes, Geometries and Styles

The form and shape of a blade play a decisive role in the purchase of a knife, and knife manufacturers do not hesitate to place great emphasis on it in their advertisements. Unfortunately, more daring and futuristic blade shapes do not always mean they are more tactically efficient. Many manufacturers simply try to get a leg up on the competition by such means.

It would go beyond the scope of this book to describe every blade shape in all their different variations. Anyway, this would be an interminable undertaking. For often it suffices to slightly lengthen a line or change a radius to change the total perception of a blade. Successful knife models are often copied by other manufacturers and sold as their own creations.

Let us limit ourselves in the following discussion to those typical blade shapes, geometries and styles that are most common in the area of tactical knives.

Shapes

Tanto

Originating from the fascinating world of Japanese blades, the Tanto shape has become almost the standard for tactical knives. The reason is that the blade point is extremely stable. The strength of the blade is great almost to the point itself, and so it can be used to pierce through solid objects without damaging the point of the blade. Tanto blades can be divided into two groups with regard to tactical knives: (1) conventionally ground on both sides, either hollow or wedge-shaped, and (2) blades ground in the shape of a chisel.

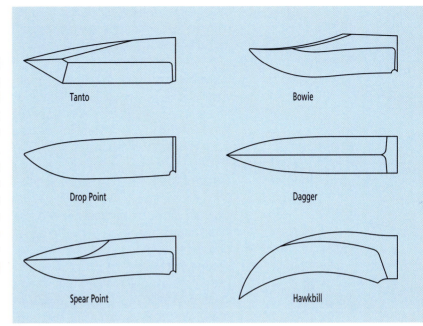

Tanto

Bowie

Drop Point

Dagger

Spear Point

Hawkbill

■ Six typical blade forms in the area of tactical knives.

Drop Point

The drop point blade actually comes from hunting and is primarily meant to be used as a tool, not as a weapon. Usually these knives do without a rear cutting edge. This is a versatile, all-purpose tool for field use.

Spear Point

The spear point shape, just like the Tanto shape, is characterized by its extreme stability in the area of the blade point. In contrast to the Bowie shape, where material is removed from the point through the radius running inward, the bulbous spear point shape is massive and resilient through the outward-running radius in the same area of the point.

Bowie

Named after the Texas patriot James Bowie and originally designed in the 19th nineteenth century as a combat knife, the Bowie blade with its classic duckbill-shaped point is likewise a good compromise between tool and weapon. The rear cutting edge can be curved or straight and generally is also sharpened. In this way, the point of the blade achieves the same effect when stabbing as the dagger shape.

Dagger

Although this book continually criticizes the dagger blade for its lack of versatility, it can indeed be used tactically. The clear advantage of the symmetrical blade can be seen in combat situations. A number of tactical maneuvers can be executed with this blade shape. One can cut upwards and outwards without having to turn the knife in the hand. If someone grabs his knife at night, he does not have to wonder where the cutting edge is. Because there are two cutting edges, pushing into material is likewise relatively easy. This is why this shape is appropriate first and foremost for stabbing. On the other hand, its usefulness as a tool is limited. Because it is ground on four sides, the blade is relatively light and unsuitable for use as a saw or crowbar. Likewise, it is impossible to exert supporting pressure on the back of the blade with the other hand.

Hawkbill

The hawkbill, i.e., sickle, shape looks more dangerous than it is. It is intended mainly for use as a tool and is excellently suited for cutting through ropes and belts. It is hardly useful at all for stabbing or precise cutting. However, its dangerousness should not be underestimated.

Geometries

Besides the shape of the blade, its geometry is a deciding factor on of its efficiency. Users should also consider beforehand what weight will might be put on the knife in the future.

Wedge Cut

The wedge or conical shape is most appropriate for blades that must withstand a lot of force from chopping or crowbarring. A cross-section view shows that it is cut in a wedge shape, as the name suggests. Material is continually built up behind the cutting edge. The relationship between the width and the strength of the blade will determine the knife's performance. The thinner the wedge, the less the material being cut needs to be moved and the better it cuts. However, a narrow blade again means less stability. On the other hand, a stronger blade with a wider wedge means greater stability, although in order to achieve reasonable cutting performance the cutting edge has to be sharpened at a steep angle. The more wear and tear is put on the cutting edge over time, the more material wears away from the point of the wedge. The result is a cutting edge that grows wider and wider, whose shine can cause undesirable reflections. Nevertheless, the wedge cut is fundamentally recommended for a knife that has to meet heavy demands. Because of modern computerized grinding factories, there are hardly any limits as to how the wedge point can be shaped.

■ **The four most popular blade shapes.**

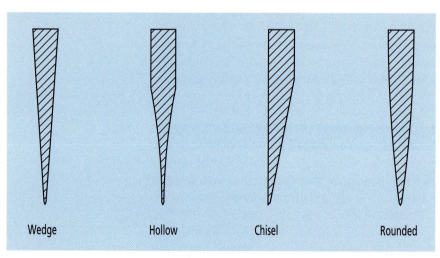

Wedge Hollow Chisel Rounded

Hollow Cut

For the hollow cut, also called the razor cut, two radii of material running inward behind the cutting edge are removed. The result is a narrow, extremely sharp cutting edge that is relatively easy to sharpen later. The disadvantage as compared to the chisel cut is its lesser stability. In rare cases, the hollow cut extends the entire length of the blade to the back. Usually the back is more massive than the hollow cut portion, which ensures the blade's basic stability. Blades should only be hollow cut if they are to be used primarily for cutting and not for chopping or crowbarring. Even if the blade does not break, the thin cutting edge can be greatly damaged.

Chisel Cut

The chisel cut is a one-sided wedge cut that can be found, for example, on Japanese chef's knives. The fact that only one side needs to be kept sharp is a decisive advantage. Knife experts are divided as to which side of the blade should be cut. If one is cutting horizontally, then it really makes no difference which side is ground. But if one wants to work with the blade away from the body, it quickly becomes a greater issue. When working with wood, a carpenter holds a chisel so that the ground side faces up, in order to remove the material. This carries over to knives designed with a chisel cut. If the user is right-handed, the cut should lie on the right side of the blade, if one is looking at it from the back of the blade. For left-handed users it is exactly the opposite. Unfortunately, the knife industry and knife makers pay far too little attention to this fact, with few exceptions such as Canadian knifemaker Greg Lightfoot.

Rounded Cut

The rounded cut is used overwhelmingly for hatchets and is very uncommon on tactical knives. One of the rare exceptions is Bill Harsey's handmade "Smatchet." This knifemaker made a very conscious decision for the rounded cut, because the knife is used primarily as a hatchet.

Construction

A knife's construction is very important in determining its stability. In the field of tactical knives, three tang shapes are prevalent.

Round Tang

The round tang runs all the way through the handle and is either screwed onto, or pinned into, the pommel. If the tang is screwed on, it is possible to re-screw it together should it become loose. If the tang is pinned in, then it is more difficult to repair the knife.

Cut Down Tang

Here, only a short piece of the tang extends into the handle and is secured by simply gluing it in or screwing or pinning it in. Typical examples of this construction method are survival knives with hollow handles.

Flat Tang

This tang either runs untapered (full tang) or tapered (tapered tang) to the end of the handle. Of all the tang forms, this one has the greatest stability.

Anyone needing a knife that can withstand the maximum amount of force should choose the so-called fully integrated construction method, in which blade, hilt, tang

Combat and Tactical Knives from a Medical Viewpoint: The Shape of the Blade and its Effect on the Enemy's Body

By Dr. Rudolph Bermel

The use of knives for self-defense and to defend one's country is as old as mankind itself. Experiences gained from hunting soon showed users which organs were vital and which parts of the body were especially vulnerable. Research in the field of anatomy and the development of surgery extended this knowledge. By using this knowledge in hand-to-hand combat, the great similarities in the position and structure of these organs in humans and animals were revealed to the successful combatant. The lungs and heart of humans and wild animals are almost completely protected by the rib cage; pushing into this area with a knife is very difficult. The neck, with its arteries and windpipe, is easy to wound and is only rarely covered by armor or something similar. However, in order to definitively injure the enemy, the length of the blade had to be sufficient, corresponding to approximately the diameter of the body. In a frontal attack, the goal was to penetrate the arteries of the stomach and/or the large veins. Both lie in front of the spinal column, hence deep inside the abdominal cavity. These blood vessels therefore enjoy maximum protection from behind over the entire length of the spine. Stabbing the heart from beneath the sternum upwards and through it was an easier way of killing the enemy.

However, it was soon recognized that double-edged blades penetrated easier and more deeply into the body. This can also be seen in the development of the combat knife. Double-ground blades were also easier to use in cutting throats, and the combatant no longer had to pay attention to which side of the blade to use on the enemy's neck. Some arms and knife makers who preferred to use a single-edged blade tried to compensate for this deficiency by using a special structure on the handle. The blade's width and thickness play an important role in penetrating the rib cage. A very wide, thick blade, even if it is extremely sharp and double-edged, can hardly get through the ribs. The elastic rib cage can also survive a violent blow. More dangerous are narrow, thin, long, double-edged knives whose diameter is smaller than that of the spaces between the ribs. This is why an ice pick or a large, sharpened screwdriver is more dangerous in this respect than a large bush knife, which really is more suited as a striking weapon.

Another characteristic of many tactical knives is the so-called "blood channel." This is a groove that is ground out parallel to the axis, which is found on daggers from the Middle Ages to contemporary times. The point here was to accelerating accelerate the enemy's bleeding if the knife got stuck in his body. Because after the knife is pushed in the sides of the wound lie closed around the blade, relatively little blood seeps out. But if the knife contains a blood channel, a great deal more blood comes

---

The author is a tactical emergency physician and colonel in the *Luftwaffe* paratroopers.

out. This fact becomes quite obvious by looking at a practical example. If you stick a knife into a closed milk carton and leave it here, only a little fluid will come out. But if you do the same thing using a knife with a blood channel, the milk carton will soon be empty. The attentive reader who is taught within the scope of first aid: "Leave the knife in the wound!" may wonder why. Well, this admonition is correct for the following reasons. By pulling it out, usually even more tissue is damaged, since you can hardly pull it out exactly the same way it was pushed in. If the point of the knife is sticking in a blood vessel, again, the sides of the wound are relatively tightly closed off so that only a little blood comes out. Also, the blood channel usually doesn't begin until far behind the knife point. By binding up the wound and carefully fixing the knife into place, the bandages also block the blood channel. However, this does not stop any internal bleeding. Thus, the highest priority must be given to providing the fastest care possible and getting the victim to a sick bay or hospital.

and pommel are made from a single piece of steel. Good examples of these are knifemaker Tom Johanning's "TAC-10" and "TAC-11" models, as well as Stefan Steigerwald's "Tactical."

Blade Materials

The heart of a knife is its blade. Tactical users expect it to be as stable as possible, stand up to some mistreatment, not rust and stay sharp forever. But however much modern research can improve the quality of the materials, compromises must be made. To be sure, slick marketing strategies in the knife industry are always claiming to have found the ultimate blade material, but there is still a long way to go before the perfect material can be found. Here are the most important knife materials and their characteristics.

Steel
Looking at the types of steels that are used in making tactical knives, it becomes apparent that each manufacturer uses different kinds, which has a lot to do with the philosophy of the individual company or knife maker. The varieties range from non rust-resistant carbon steels ("tool steel") to classic stainless steels to powdered metallurgical steels. The specific characteristics of each type of steel determine the purpose for which it is used. Thus, a non rust-resistant carbon steel is certainly not used for maritime tactical knives. Thus, before choosing the type of steel to be used, the manufacturer must definitely know the conditions under which the knife will later be used later. Unalloyed steel with a carbon content of a maximum of 1.7 percent is distinguished from alloyed steel containing additional elements besides carbon, such as chromium, molybdenum, vanadium, manganese, etc., which contribute their individual qualities. Through a special process, powdered metallurgical steel can have a carbon content of up to 2.2 percent.

The most important knife steel alloy components

Description	C %	Cr %	Mo %	V %
Non rust-resistant steels				
1095	0.9-1.03			
A-2 (1.2363)	0.9-1.05	4.75-5.5	0.9-1.4	0.4
O-1 (1.2510)	0.85-0.95	0.2-0.6		0.05-0.15
L-6	0.75	0.90	0.35	
Rust-resistant steels				
420-J2 (1.4034)	0.42-0.5	12.5-14.5		
440-A (1.4110)	0.48-0.6	13.0-15.0	0.5-0.8	0.15
440-B (1.4112)	0.85-0.95	17.0-19.0	0.9-1.3	0.07-0.12
440-C (1.4125)	0.95-1.2	16.0-18.0	0.4-0.8	
D-2 (1.2379)	1.55	11.0-12.5	0.6-0.8	1.1
12-C-27	0.6	13.5-14.5		
AUS-6	0.55-0.65	13.5-14.5		0.1-0.3
AUS-8	0.7-0.8	13.5-14.5	0.1-0.3	0.1-0.3
BG-42	1.15	14.5	4.0	1.3
ATS-34	0.95-1.05	13.5-14.5	3.5-4.0	
154CM	1.05	14.0	4.0	
X-15 T.N	0.4	15.5	2.0	0.3
VG-10	0.95-1.05	14.5-15.5	0.9-1.2	0.1-0.3
Stellite 6 K	1.6	28	1.0	
Talonite	0.9-1.4	28-32	1.5	
Powdered metallurgical steels				
CPM-T-420-V	2.2	13.3	1.2	9.1
CPM-T-440-V	2.2	17.5	0.5	5.75

This table lists only the currently most commonly used steels for tactical knives and does not claim to be comprehensive.

Carbon is the most important element of steel. Steel is considered hardened if it contains at least 0.4 percent carbon. Increased carbon content raises the hardness of the blade and the formation of carbides. Carbides are extremely hard and are the result of chemical compounds that occur when the excess carbon reacts with other alloy components such as chromium or vanadium. Steel has greater cutting ability the more carbides it contains, but that does make it more difficult to sharpen. When the percentage of carbon reaches 2.3 percent, steel becomes cast iron.

Mn %	Si %	P %	Ni %	W %	Co %	N %	HRc
0.3-0.5	0.1	0.04					58-60
0.45-0.75	0.5						58-60
1.0-1.4	0.1-0.4			0.4-0.6			58-60
0.75			1.75				60-61
1.0	1.0						54-55
1.0	1.0						56
1.0	1.0		0.3				56-58
1.0	1.0						58-60
0.15-0.45	0.3						60-62
0.35-0.4	0.35-0.4						54-56
1.0	1.0						56
0.8-1.0	1.0						58
0.5	0.3						59-61
0.6	0.35						59-61
0.6	0.3						59-61
						0.2	58
0.5	0.6	0.3			1.3-1.5		58-60
2.0	2.0		3.0	4.5	60.0		46-47
2.0	2.0		3.0	3.5-5.5	60.0		46-47
0.5	0.5						58-60
0.5	0.5						58-60

Figures for alloy components may vary according to manufacturer or analysis.

Chromium, if it is available in sufficient quantities, protects against corrosion. Once the chromium content reaches 13.4 percent, steel may be called rustproof. Most steels are at best rust-resistant and begin to rust depending on how long they are exposed to the elements. With an increased chromium content, the structure becomes a very hard chromium carbide.

Molybdenum is a general steel refiner and can be found with a content of 4 percent in such popular steels as ATS-34, 154CM and BG-42. Moreover, molybdenum raises steel's resistance to corrosion as well as its toughness, because it creates a homogeneous distribution of chromium within the structure. In addition, it cultivates the uniform hardness and overall strength of the steel.

Vanadium supports the formation of carbides and creates a very fine-pored structure that results in a good cutting ability and resistance to heat. Powdered metallurgical steels like CPM-T-440-V and CPM-T-420-V have a vanadium content of between 5.75 percent and 9.1 percent.

Manganese likewise increases the toughness of steel and its mechanical qualities.

Silicon increases steel's resilience. However, the steelmaker must be careful not to mix in too much of this element, otherwise the structure will become brittle.

A very important factor in determining steel's cutting ability is, of course, its **hardness**, which is measured in HRc (Hardness Rockwell Cone). It is measured by pressing a diamond piece into the steel at a defined pressure. The Rockwell hardness of modern blade steels is between 54 and 62 HRc. The hardness requirement for each individual type of steel depends on the alloys and their cutting abilities. Through selective hardening, the blade's efficacy can be improved even more. In this process, the cutting edge has a higher Rockwell hardness than the back of the blade. This happy union combines an extremely hard, sharp and cutting blade with a flexible, more resilient back. However, this only works with non-rustproof steels that do not contain chromium. One of the few manufacturers to use this process, Mad Dog Knives, introduced the process with a partial series of knives under the brand name "Starret 496-01." The cutting blade has a Rockwell hardness of 62 HRc and the back between 50 and 54 HRc. An alternative method of selective hardening is the

■ **In spite of their great tendency to corrode, Lile Handmade Knives are popular because of the excellent cutting ability of D-2 steel. Shown here is the "Deathwind" model.**

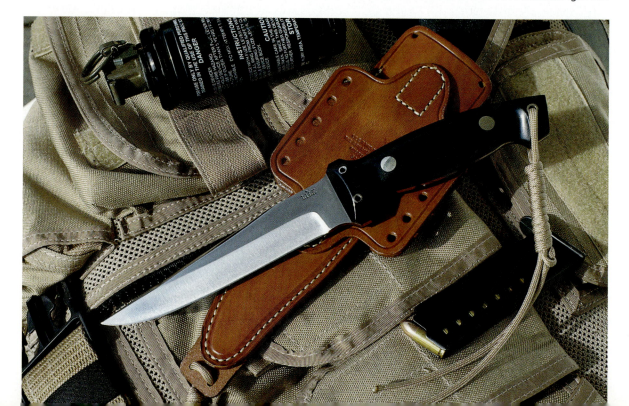

use of the three-layered steel "San Mai III," which, in contrast to "Starret 496-01," has the additional advantage of being resistant to corrosion in the field. Cold Steel's use of "San Mai III" imbeds a core of Japanese AUS-8 steel between to two 420J2 steels. With a carbon content of 0.7-0.8 percent, the hardness of the AUS-8 is still 58 HRc, while the 420J2, with a carbon content of 0.42-0.5 percent only reaches 54 HRc and is thus softer. The result is a flexible blade with a hard cutting edge.

The most important question with regard to steel continues to be: "Which type is most appropriate for tactical knives?" Experts often get into heated discussions about this, and their opinions could not be more different. Leading knifemakers who have made a name for themselves in the field of tactical knives have taken the following positions.

Allen Elishewitz places great value on cutting ability and shock absorption as well as resistance to corrosion, and for this reason he chooses Crucible Steel's rustproof 154CM, the brand name of the Japanese ATS-34, for his blades for field use as well as for urban enemies. Bill Harsey is of the same opinion. He also values steel according to its resistance to corrosion and cutting ability under extreme conditions. Harsey truly understands the effect of salt water in maritime use, because it can corrode a blade into dullness before it is even taken out of its sheath. Therefore, he categorically rejects non-rustproof carbon steels. To get the most out of the 154CM, which he praises highly, he pays strict attention to the exact hardness requirements. He sees as the wave of the future powdered metallurgical steels with enormous cutting ability, but in his opinion they are too expensive for making knives. The most innovative maker of tactical knives, Bob Terzuola, also swears by 154CM. For him, the relationship between the cost and utility of this steel is unsurpassable. He feels that powdered metallurgical steels have clear advantages in the way of their cutting ability, but the problems of working the steel and the high cost of the materials do not make it worthwhile for manufacturing large quantities. According to Terzuola, non-rustproof steels should absolutely not be used for flick-blade knives.

Canadian Wally Hayes has a completely different philosophy; he prefers the non-rustproof carbon steel 0-1. He sees an advantage in the possibility of selectively hardening the blade with a flexible back and a hard cutting edge. In his opinion, the structure of the cutting edge, which offers great sharpness, is finer than with a rustproof alloy. So that his blades can also be used in maritime areas, he gives them a simple coating of Kalgard. Charles Ochs shares this viewpoint, and likewise uses E-52100 carbon steel for his knives. Steven Dick, chief editor of the journal *Tactical*

■ **William Harsey sharpening a titanium spring for the "A-F" folding knife. According to this knifemaker, the blade of a tactical knife should be made from stainless steel.**

Knives, likewise sees an enormous advantage in terms of sharpness with carbon steels like A-2, 0-1 and 1095. Of course, it must be taken into consideration that these blades will rust if not cared for properly.

The following conclusion can be taken away from these diverse points of view: Both carbon steels and rustproof steel alloys have their place in the field of tactical knives. Both have their advantages and disadvantages depending on how they are to be used, and the user must weigh these.

Cobalt-based alloys

So-called cobalt-based alloys were developed for heavily used parts in airplane turbines that have to withstand extreme mechanical stress, high temperatures and heavy corrosion. These are malleable alloys with a very high carbon content, in which iron is replaced by cobalt. The material has a maximum hardness of 47 HRc and cannot be made any harder. Because of this maximum hardness, it takes a long time to produce a blade. Knifemaker Harold Carson once called this material "grinder eater." The advantages are its enormous resistance to corrosion, as well as its resistance to wear and tear when cutting relatively soft materials like meat, wood and nautical rigging. High pressure through impact is a problem because the when the blade meets hard materials, it simply bends. So again, its usage has to fit with the tasks it is required to accomplish. Two of the most well-known cobalt-based alloys are Stellite 6K and Talonite. In recent years, Rob Simonich has strongly promoted Talonite in the knife scene. Camillus and T.O.P.S. are some of the few industrial knife manufacturers to use this material. The sale price of these knives is still quite high compared to their counterparts with regular steel blades.

Titanium

Titanium is an oxide found in the minerals rutile and ilmenite. It is the ninth most common element in the earth's crust and can be found in most volcanic rocks. Australia is the world's leading producer of titanium. Commercially pure titanium consists of 99 to 99.7 percent titanium; the rest is comprised of nitrogen, oxygen, carbon and tungsten. The most outstanding qualities of titanium have already been discussed in the section on handle materials on page 136, and the same qualities make it valuable for making blades. The most serious difference, however, is the titanium alloys that are used for blades. As opposed to the 6Al-6V alloy which is used for handles, shells and locks, beta titanium is used to make blades. Beta titanium consists of more than 75 percent titanium; the rest is comprised of a mixture of aluminum, vanadium, chromium and molybdenum. Beta titanium is harder than any other titanium alloy available. As a comparison, pure titanium has a Rockwell hardness of 25 HRc; 6A1-6C has a hardness of 34 HRc, and beta titanium has a hardness of 47 HRc. Compared to high-quality knife steels that are generally between 56 and 61 HRc, 47 HRc is seems rather low. However, it must be considered that a direct comparison is impossible because these materials are so different from one another. Moreover, because of its solid structure, titanium's resilience is significantly greater. Certainly, titanium is one of the most demanding materials

to work with. Titanium is a very poor conductor of heat. Anyone working with titanium in an industrial setting who has to sharpen a titanium knife will soon discover that sharpening it at high temperatures leads to an undesirable distortion of the blade. Special tools and a sharpener that is tailored to the material are needed to be able to produce a smooth blade. American and Japanese companies bring their expertise to this area. Mission Knives offers the largest selection of tactical knives with titanium blades, and for some years they have also sold a flick-blade knife ("MPF") composed entirely of titanium. Warren Thomas is the titanium king among knifemakers.

Titanium carbide alloys have an even greater cutting ability than beta titanium. Powdered metallurgical production processes make this possible: using a sintering (heating without melting) process, the soft titanium structure is combined with carbides with a Vickers hardness of more than 3,000 (off the Rockwell hardness scale). Just as with steel, carbides multiply the cutting ability of titanium many times over. One of the first international companies to offer knives with titanium carbide blades was the Solingen company Böker.

Ceramic
As early as the 1980s, knives with ceramic blades appeared on the market, first for cooking knives, and then as general-use flick-blade knives. Concerning ceramic as a blade material, it is necessary to differentiate between normal ceramic, which everyone recognizes from crockery and which is composed of clay, feldspar and water, and technical ceramic, which is synthetically produced from inorganic materials like aluminum oxide, silicone carbide, silicone nitrite and zircon oxide.

■ In the field of titanium blades, Mission Knives is the undisputed market leader.

Zircon oxide (ZrO_2) is best suited for blades, because it has the most flexibility and thereby minimizes the risk of breakage for the blade and cutting edge. A precise quantity of zircon oxide is pressed together with a binding material in a metal blade formed under high pressure and is then sintered. During the sintering process, the minute particles are first fused together, and then they are formed back into a knife blank. The advantages of a ceramic blade are obvious: it does not corrode, it does not conduct electricity, it is extremely wear-resistant, it is extraordinarily hard, it is relatively light and it is anti-magnetic.

The disadvantages are that it is easily breakable by hard shocks, and it is relatively difficult to re-sharpen. But again, the decision for or against a ceramic blade should be made depending on what tasks it needs to fulfill. Certainly for bomb squads who have to dismantle bombs and mines that can detonate by being magnetized, a ceramic blade is not the worst choice, indeed, it is indispensable. Of course, knives with ceramic blades are also offered to maritime users.

Some manufacturers of tactical knives with ceramic blades are Mad Dog, with its "Mirage X" series, and Böker, with its "Infinity" model. Thus far, the only handmade knives with ceramic blades are offered by Bob Terzuola

Synthetic Material

In the area of synthetic material, the duroplastic material G-10, which has already been discussed in the section about handle materials on page 133, is most prevalent with knifemakers and industrial manufacturers. The advantage of using G-10 as a blade material is, first of all, the simple mechanics of forming it by grinding and sharpening. But the cutting ability of synthetic material should not be too highly estimated, even though this group of materials is well-known for its enormous stability. The cutting ability can be improved by adding serration, although the blade then rips more than it actually cuts. For this reason, blades made out of synthetic materials are mostly used for stabbing. Mission Knives, with its "Counter Terrorist" series, has cornered the international market, as it has with its titanium-blade knives. Likewise, several other companies offer knives with synthetic blades. But these are

■ **The Böker "Infinity" with ceramic blade. Because of the metal parts in the handle, this knife is still somewhat magnetic and so is not really suitable for members of bomb squads.**

Industrial or Handmade Knives?

This question is no longer that easy to answer. Although years ago the distinction was easy to make because of differences in quality and in the corresponding prices, the use of computerized production plants has narrowed the gap between industrial and handmade knives. Even the extremely high-quality steels that used only to be found on handmade knives, such as the powdered metallurgical steel CPM-T-440-V or D-2 steel, are now part of the natural repertoire of any well-known industrial knife manufacturer. Knifemakers often furnish large manufacturers with designs of their well-known models: Bob Terzuola for Spyderco, Walter Brend for Böker, Greg Lightfoot...the list could go on and on. In general, knifemakers are quite happy to find a manufacturer who will build their designs under license. This frees up more time for them to dream up new projects, and offers income supplemented by regular royalties.

The purchase of a handmade knife gains meaning if it is the realization of an individual design. If someone simply cannot find the right knife on the market that he desperately needs to do the job, there is always the possibility of having an individual piece made by hand. This is the unbeatable advantage of the knifemaker, because he is very happy to accommodate his customers' wishes. Often knifemakers can do things that are technically impossible for even computerized production plants to accomplish. However, the individuality of such pieces comes at a high cost of time and money, and this means a good income for the knifemaker. Coming to the heart of the matter: A tactical knife is a utilitarian object that wears out and can get lost. If the knife is not provided by the employer as an official piece of equipment, it is up to the user to decide for himself what price he is willing to pay for it. If an employer does not provide a knife as an official piece of equipment, it is up to the user to decide what price he is willing to pay for it.

◾ **Above: Left, Böker's "Brend" model, manufactured as part of a series; right, the handmade original from Walter Brend—same design, different production techniques, materials and pricing.**

◾ **Right: Members of the Canadian special forces, the ERT, purchased knifemaker Wally Hayes' handmade models "TAC 1" and "TAC Custom" with their own funds.**
Photo: Wally Hayes/Norm Goulet

mostly based on thermoplastic materials like ABS or polyamide, which again are produced using a relatively expensive spray-on process. Examples of these are Cold Steel's "CAT Tanto" model and Lansky Sharpeners' "The Knife."

Serrated Edges and Teeth

Since 1982, when Spyderco brought its "Mariner" model on the market, serrated edges and teeth havve become typical features of tactical knives, regardless of whether they are fixed-blade or flick-blade knives. But even here there is a range of differences, mainly in the form of the serration and its position on the blade. The following section explains what the essential advantages are of serration and the philosophies behind the various forms.

The advantage of a serrated edge over a flat edge is in the considerably longer, linear cutting edge that results from the radii of the serration. If the radii of the serration are added together, the cutting edge is actually longer than the blade itself. But even more important is that fact that each point of the serration grabs the material afresh and tears into it. The force is thus concentrated on the points, which—proportional to the force being used—again leads to a greater depth of the cut in contrast to that accomplished by a flat blade. The points also ensure that the indentations on the cutting edge are better protected and stay sharp longer. The protected parts of the cutting blade inside the radius also cannot be bent as easily as the cutting edge of a flat blade, which also helps the knife stay sharp longer.

Cutting depth depends strongly on the form, size and angle of the serration. Usually there is one large radius followed by two small ones. The resulting points can either be sharp or rounded off. Spyderco, Micro Tech and Gerber produce examples of sharp serrations. Round serrations can be found on models from Mission Knives and KA-BAR. Experts disagree as to which form is better. The fact is that sharp serrations are more aggressive; they rip and achieve maximum cutting depth by the use of great force. Round serrations, on the other hand, cut more than rip. A more-even, less-splintery cut is advantageous with very fibrous materials like ropes and nautical rigging.

Just as with the form of the serration, there are differing points of view as to which side of the blade should contain the serration. When cutting vertically, this does not matter. However, if someone is cutting away from his body, which is always recommended for reasons of safety, then the serration should be on the right side of the blade (viewed from the back) if he is right-handed so that he has the ideal cutting angle. A view from the handle to a cross-section of the blade shows that the serration runs diagonally from the top right to the bottom left. The lower left side creates the cutting angle, which always meets the material being cut from both a shallow angle and a steep angle, just like a chisel. The material is then forced upwards. We are already familiar with this issue from our discussion of the chisel-shaped Tanto blades (see page 147). Spyderco founder Sal Glesser, on the other hand, is of the opinion that a right-sided serration makes the blade move to the left during cutting. In the early 1980s, experiments with household knives supposedly led him to this conclusion. Since he saw the danger that housewives would cut themselves in the hand during cooking and launch an avalanche of product-related lawsuits, he decided to put his serration on the left side of the blade. And that is how all Spyderco models are made even today. However, the observant knife aficionado may well ask himself the question, how many Spyderco knives are actually used in the kitchen?

Then there are teeth. These are, quite simply, evenly spaced breaks on the cutting edge whose corners are designed to better grab the material being cut. Compared to serrated blades, toothed blades have more-modest cutting results. Toothed blades tear and splinter the material being cut. But they can be relatively easily re-sharpened in the field on a flat stone. The best example of a toothed blade can be found on Böker's "A-F" knife. Colonel Applegate, who deeply detested serrated blades, once told the author: "True warriors don't bring kitchen knives into battle!"

Experts are again divided into two camps on the best way to re-sharpen a serrated blade. Some think that each individual radius should be worked with a narrow, conical sharpening steel from front to back. On the other hand, others advise sharpening the serration with a flat stone from front to back.

As was said before, the philosophies regarding serrated edges clash strongly and irreconcilably.

■ Left, a left-sided, sharply serrated edge from Micro Tech; right, a right-sided, blunted serrated edge from Mission Knives.

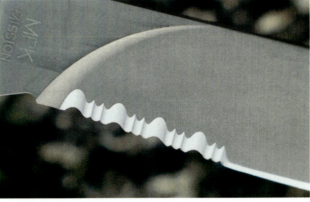

Types of Surface Treatments

From a psychological standpoint, one might think that a shiny blade would have a demoralizing effect on an enemy in hand-to-hand combat and give its owner a tactical advantage. However, anyone who is ordered to use his knife—as an alternative to a silencer—as a silent weapon in an emergency will certainly prefer a matte blade. For this will in no way betray him by reflecting light. This, of course, applies to tactical operations as well as to the use of the knife as a tool.

Nowadays, (most) manufacturers are putting increasingly more thought into the area of surface treatments. Besides making the surface matte, hardening the surface and protecting it against corrosion are gaining in importance. There are two basic types of processes that can be distinguished: changing the surface by a mechanical process or by means of a coating.

Mechanical surface treatments

Satinizing
In the satinizing process, the surface is given a hatched appearance by means of brushes or grinding machines. The bigger the grain size, the more matter the surface becomes. The hatching can be brought about mechanically or by hand with sandpaper, as many knifemakers prefer. The blade does become matte, but it still reflects direct rays of light.

Stone-washing
With the stone-washed method the blade is—in the truest sense of the word—washed, i.e., polished, by vibrating it between stones with grinding materials. As with satinizing, the size of the stones, the grinding materials and the amount of time determine the appearance of the surface, which is matte, irregularly patterned and rather resistant. But it, too, reflects light unfavorably.

Spraying
This is the easiest method of making a blade matte. Particles are sprayed onto the blade's surface under high pressure. These particles can consist of corundum or glass beads, depending on the composition of the surface and how gray a color is desired. Spraying with corundum rubs off a lot of the surface, which leads to the creation of more rust. Glass beads make the surface thicker and more resistant to corrosion. Sprayed surfaces scratch relatively quickly.

Surface Coatings
In contrast to mechanical surface treatments, only one coat is applied. According to the type of coating, this can result in not only a matte appearance, but also protection against corrosion or extreme resilience. Coating costs can also be quite variable. While a powdered or lacquered coating is rather inexpensive, hard coatings made with titanium aluminum nitrides can raise costs considerably. Not every coating process is automatically suited to every blade. If the coating temperature exceeds

the acceptable temperature of the blade, the blade will lose its hardness. So the temperature cannot climb too high.

■ With the "stone-washed" method, the blades are polished by vibrating them between stones with grinding materials.

Powdered and lacquered coatings

Because of their very different qualities, coatings should be chosen in accordance with the quality of the blade steel and how the blade will be used. Powdered and lacquered coatings are used most with non-rustproof steel alloys. The coating completely covers the steel and protects it from the elements. Of course, the cutting edge, from which the coating must be removed after the process, is the weak point. It is still susceptible to corrosion.

Powdered and lacquered coatings rub off a lot more easily than hard coatings. In terms of cost, however, it is an inexpensive method of blackening steel blades and at the same time protecting them against corrosion. Chris Reeve Knives, Becker Knife & Tool, Ontario, Cold Steel, Columbia River Knife & Tool and KA-BAR, to name a few, have used this method for years. One of the most common types of powdered coatings is powdered epoxy or Teflon-S. Through an electroplating process, the powdered particles are added onto the blade and then baked on. Unfortunately, the coat usually is quite thick, which does not make the corners and edges look very good. On the other hand, Kalgard is a lacquer that is applied onto the surface with a spraying apparatus. The thickness of the coating is much better regulated. After applying the lacquer coating, the blade is placed in an approximately 160

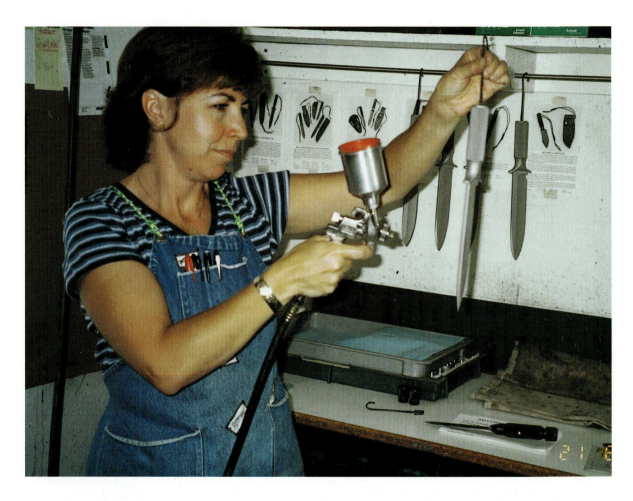

■ **An employee of the knife manufacturer Chris Reeves Knives covers a survival knife, which has already been sand-sprayed, with Kalgard.**

degrees Celsius oven for an hour, whereby the lacquer particles bake into a solid coat.

Hard Coatings

For knives with high-quality, rust-proof steel, the coating plays an essential role as protection against corrosion. Furthermore, it is a matter of arming the surface against wear and tear and scratches. In the mid-1990s, the first American knife manufacturer began to treat its blades with a process called "physical vapor deposition" ("PVD"). This process is mainly found in the area of tool technology, for example in coating grinders and drills that are used to file metal and other materials that are difficult to file, and also in the technical area of pressing, pulling, and bending metals. Although usually these coatings are gold-colored, they can also be black or gray. The most well-knownwell known hard coatings are titanium carbon nitride (TiCN), titanium aluminum nitride (TiAlN) and chromium nitride (CrN).

Besides having an extremely resilient, black surface, hard coatings serve another very important function, of which few manufacturers take advantage: Coating tools extends their lifespan, and the same effect can be imparted to the cutting edge of a knife. If a highly sharpened knife is coated, its life can be greatly extended. Coating creates a minimal, but perceptible diminishment in sharpness. Sharpening the cutting edge on one side only can compensate for this; in this way the hard coating on the other side of the blade is undisturbed. When re-sharpening the blade later, one should be careful always to sharpen the same side.

Tactical Carrying Possibilities and Systems

Besides the knives themselves, systems for carrying them have developed significantly in recent decades. Although for a long time the emphasis was placed on securely carrying knives on a belt around the waist, it had already been shown during WWII and later in Vietnam that there were alternative and more-sensible ways of attaching knives. Members of special forces popularized the method of carrying sheaths on the belt with the opening upside down. But because most sheaths at the time did not have the corresponding fasteners, the soldiers soon made use of duct tape and cords. Randall Made Knives was one of the first companies to react to this need by fitting its models Models 14, 15 and 18 with sheaths having additional fastener holes in the belt loops at their disposal.

Tactical carrying systems underwent a huge push in development in the late 1980s. The recognition that the user not only had to carry his knife securely, but also had to be able to attach it in a number of ways, and furthermore

■ **Sheaths made out of Kydex, Hytrel, Cordura, and leather.**

pull it out at lightning speed, made the use of modern materials whose functionality was far superior to that of old-fashioned leather unavoidable. The thermoplastic synthetic material Kydex, made by Kleerdex, became an icon of thermoplastic sheaths. There are hardly any major manufacturers who do not offer sheaths made out of this material. In addition to Kydex, polyamide and ABS are also utilized, using an injection molding process mainly when the desire is to manufacture the greatest number of pieces at the lowest possible cost or where metal parts are undesirable on the sheath, as with divers' knives, for example.

DuPont's Cordura is used for knife sheaths as well as folding knife cases; it is impossible to imagine the field of tactical knives without it.

What distinguishes the individual materials, what their advantages and disadvantages are, which types of knives they are especially suited for and how they are made – all this will all be covered in the sections to that follow.

Leather

Leather is one of the oldest sheath materials *par excellence,* and even today it is still often used to make tactical sheaths. But it needs to be a high-quality leather that is as strong and sturdy as possible. Leather that is too thin gives the sheath too little stability and presents the risk that the blade will pierce through it. Leather is a good-looking material, it is usually dyed black for tactical use, and it feels relatively comfortable as well. A talented knife or sheath maker can cater to his customer's customers' special requests relatively easily without having to expend too much time and effort. In addition, repairs are quite easy to manage under field conditions. From a tactical standpoint, the fact that a knife can be pulled out of a leather sheath without making noise is an advantage that is not to be taken lightly. Furthermore, leather sheaths don't make as many tell-tale noises as their synthetic counterparts when they collide with other pieces of equipment or weapons. When knives have to be worn concealed, leather is far more comfortable to wear than synthetic materials. Putting a layer of leather at the tip of the blade between the top and bottom parts of the leather sheath is particularly important. This stops the blade from cutting through the stitching. Moreover, the stitching should be done with special waterproof thread to avoid moisture absorption.

On the other hand, leather has a number of disadvantages. A leather sheath can lose its shape and fit through environmental influences like moisture, heat and cold. If it gets completely soaked through, it requires time to dry out. Furthermore, leather sheaths can only withstand the effects of piercing, cutting and scratching up to a certain point. After just a short period of use, the sheath can look really shabby. Removing sand particles and pebbles from the soft leather interior is often extremely difficult to accomplish, because cleaning a sheath with water is not advised as it only makes matters worse. If non-stainless steel blades are used, or if knives are left in their sheaths too long, corrosion problems can arise because of tannic acids in the leather or accumulated moisture.

Leather sheaths that are carried by pilots or paratroopers should have added reinforcements of synthetic material or metal to avoid being stuck through with the blade in a hard landing.

Leather cases for folding knives are becoming more and more obsolete due to the almost universal acceptance of trouser clips. However, if someone does decide on a leather case, he should make sure that the leather is strong enough to hold the knife as securely as possible. For no matter if the case is carried horizontally or vertically on the belt or other part of the uniform, there is always the chance that the flap will open and the knife will fall out. Besides, the life of leather cases is limited because they are constantly being rubbed up against clothing and subjected to the body heat of the wearer. Open leather belt holsters for folding knives are likewise available. They lie relatively close to the body, so they are comfortable to wear. Nevertheless, care should be taken to ensure that the knife is securely fastened.

Cordura

In the early 1980s, people began talking about a highly durable synthetic weave called Cordura as a sheath material. A registered trademark of the chemical giant DuPont, it is made out of 6.6 nylon, which can withstand astonishingly high temperatures of more than 260 degrees Celsius. The advantages of Cordura include durability, resistance to breaking and rubbing, and resistance to fading from UV light. Originally intended for motorcycle safety clothing, today it is used extensively for tactical vests, backpacks, boots and other pieces of equipment with pockets and belts. Of course, it is also used for tactical knife sheaths. Cordura has the additional advantage of being available in a rainbow of colors, so that the sheath can match the uniform or the job at hand. The most popular Cordura colors for tactical uniforms are black, olive green, and beige; in addition, there is a range of geography-specific camouflage patterns. The Gerber company was one of the first knife manufacturers to use Cordura as a sheath material, both in black and in "Woodland," the camouflage pattern used in the American army.

Cordura can be sewn, just like leather. But here the similarities end. As a material, Cordura is much too soft to be used as a sheath material to protect a blade adequately. Thus, for knives with fixed blades there has to be solid foundation to lend a basic shape to the sheath. The kinds of materials used for this foundation are extremely varied, ranging from manmade materials to leather to cardboard. Naturally, manmade materials offer the best protection because of their hardness. This reliably stops the blade from cutting through the sheath. Moreover, it makes it possible to use clean water to clean out the sheath when it gets dirty. Distortion because of inadequate waterproofness is not a problem. If the foundation is made out of leather or, worse yet, a cardboard-like material, then the sheath can lose its shape upon contact with water and thereby become unusable. So that moisture does not collect in the sheath for a long time, there should definitely be a small opening on the bottom end so that water can flow out and air can circulate. Good Cordura sheaths with synthetic foundations are produced by companies like

Blackhawk and S & S Systems and by knifemakers like Walter Brend. These sheaths often come with a number of optional fasteners like loops, fastener holes or clips, which makes them particularly interesting for tactical use.

The foundations of sheaths for folding knives are of less importance. Of course, here as well the material should be strong enough to be able to hold the knife securely. Some manufacturers equip their cases with an additional inner lining to protect the knife even further from piercing through. Good Cordura cases should be able to be worn both horizontally and vertically. If someone cannot find a Cordura case for his folding knife in the knife accessory section, he can find one through the numerous manufacturers of tactical magazine cases. Depending on the size of the knife, Cordura cases for single-breasted magazines fit, or one of the length-adjustable cases, such as the Blackhawk company offers, can be tried.

Well-made Cordura sheaths or cases are recognizable by darts and double stitching on the corners, among other things. These stop the sheath from opening up at these highly stressed areas.

Kydex

■ **Making handmade Kydex sheaths. The knife is first placed between two heated sheets of Kydex (left). Then the sheets of Kydex are pressed into the shape of the knife (right).**

Photo: Ernst-Wilhelm Felix-Dalichow

Kydex is a thermoplastic synthetic material based on a compound of acrylic and polyvinylchloride (PVC), which is enormously shockproof and resilient, besides being fire-resistant. Thus Kydex is used primarily to cover the interiors of airplanes and to make electronic parts. This material can be molded at a temperature as low as 180 degrees Celsius, in addition to having good contours and details. After a few knifemakers became aware of this sheath material in the 1980s, ten years still had to pass until, in the mid-1990s, the knife industry became convinced of the range of uses for Kydex.

Besides its special resilience to environmental forces and shock, the Kydex sheath offers outstanding protection for the blade. It is virtually impossible for the blade to

pierce through the sheath. It is also very easy to clean a dirty sheath under running water. But the most important argument for the Kydex sheath is the fact that the knife can be secured without a loop. The opening of the sheath can be formed so that the handle stops at a predetermined depth and can be released by the spring action of the material.

Production goes something like this: Sheets of Kydex are heated until pliable and are pressed into the shape of a knife. For the Kydex to keep its shape, pressure must be applied until the material has cooled. Otherwise, the Kydex would stretch and lose its shape. Finally, holes are bored into the sheath for the rivets that hold the sheath together. For smaller knives, glue is often sufficient. Depending on the sheath opening, after the sheath has been cooled and riveted, the knife will fit very tightly in the sheath and will be hard to pull out. The place where the handle fits is partially heated with a blast of hot air and adjusted. This procedure is good for knives that are manufactured individually or in small lots. For mass production, Kydex is poured over a form that corresponds to the contours of the knife. It is necessary that the knife form is not the least bit altered, which is hardly a problem anymore, thanks to the use of CNC-controlled manufacturing plants. However, if it has to be worked on by hand after mass production, then it must be adjusted, just like with individually-madeindividually made sheaths. The user must be able to pull his knife from the sheath with one smooth motion. The proper adjustments are very important here. Should the knife be too tightly enclosed in the sheath, the user will constantly be yanking at his equipment or belt. In the case of concealed knives, which are usually worn with the handle down in the inside coat pocket, a too-tight sheath could mean that the user ends up with a ripped pocket, and the consequences could be fatal if he discovers he is holding a sheathed knife in his hand. On the other hand, if the knife is too loose in the sheath, it can easily be lost.

The rivets that secure the upper and lower halves of the Kydex sheath are used together with a nylon cord for many functions. Slits that are etched lengthwise in between the rivets increase the number of ways the knife can be carried, if upper or lower thigh belts are available.

Unfortunately, Kydex also scratches blades and handles. Moreover, if particles of

■ **U.S. knifemaker Bud Nealy critically inspects an industrially molded Kydex sheet for his "MCS" sheath system at the Böker company. Behind him is Böker's head of construction, Franz-Josef Heimann.**

dirt get lodged into the sheath, this could lead to serious damage to the surface of the blade. From a tactical standpoint, the rather loud clicking that can be heard when pulling out or putting away the knife can be undesirable. Kydex sheaths can hardly be repaired under field conditions. Likewise, in severe heat conditions, for example in desert regions, the sheath can lose its shape.

Although it is overwhelmingly used for knives with fixed blades, Kydex is being used more and more for folding knives. Generally these sheaths are made by manufacturers specializing in individually made and limited-series knives. Here again, an advantage is that the knife can be pulled out quickly without having to open the latch on a case.

■ **Polyamide sheaths can be used for other special purposes because of their durability; here, in connection with using the blade as a screwdriver.**

For a few years now, the Blade-Tech company has been offering sheaths made out of Concealex as well. According to Tim Wegner, the head of Blade-Tech, Concealex has the same properties as Kydex, but is available in different colors and camouflage patterns.

Sprayed-on materials

Besides being able to be cast in forms, sheaths can also be made using a spray-on process. The materials that are used for this are likewise thermoplastic synthetic materials that are characterized by their enormous resilience and unbreakability. Producing such sheaths is similar to the production of thermoplastic handles, as discussed on page 131. The most common materials are polyamide (PA) and acrylonitril-butadine-styrol (ABS).

Sheaths made out of synthetic materials are distinctive in that they protect against being pierced through by the knife, and they are easily cleaned with clear water. Depending on how the sheath is made, additional metal parts like push buttons and rivets can also be added on. This is especially useful where knives and sheaths are subject to a great risk of corrosion, as in maritime use. Indeed, there is also a whole range of sheaths that open using a spring system, to stop the knife even without a safety latch and at the same time stop the blade from rattling around in the sheath. The constant force of the springs can, however, leave unintended scratch marks on the surface when pulling it out and putting it away.

Sheaths made of synthetic materials offer a number of technical possibilities than cannot be accomplished by other materials. Thus, rather complicated stopping mechanisms can be easily built into the sheath. The example of the combination screwdriver/knife sheath shows that it is even wholly possible to use a sheath as a tool. Moreover, synthetic material protects against electrical currents, for which the buyer is surely thankful when cutting through electrical lines. Multifunctional attachment devices can be easily installed on sheaths made of thermoplastic synthetic materials by using a spray-on process, resulting in no need for additional assembly.

Some of the disadvantages of synthetic material sheaths, as already discussed in the Kydex section, are the inability to make repairs under exigent conditions and the undesirable sounds that occur when they come into contact with weapons or other pieces of equipment. From a production standpoint, the high cost of initially creating the tools can be criticized. Also, changing the forms later can only be done with great difficulty and great financial expenditures.

Folding Knives

In the area of folding knives, the trouser or belt clip is predominant. Spyderco's founder, Sal Glesser, popularized it as early as the 1980s. However, his attempt to patent this carrying system failed. Therefore, today nearly all folding knife manufacturers offer models with clips. The shapes of the clips and their assembly can be very different. By and large, using two or three Phillips, six-sided, or torque screws, is prevalent, and the clip is sometimes also placed behind the screw head of the blade housing. But much more important than the way it is screwed together is how it is arranged. Here, two nearly completely opposed positions have been developed among users. The first group thinks that the clip must be mounted to the end of the handle so that when grasped, the knife is lying in the right direction in the hand without having to rearrange it. This thesis is supported by the fact that the catchline is also located on the end of the handle and makes pulling it out easier. This method is called "tip up carry." If the blade is not properly closed, however, these this carrying method is potentially dangerous. Grasping the knife can result in severe injuries.

The other side is of the opinion that the clip should be fastened to the top side of the knife ("tip down carry"). When the owner reaches into his pocket to pull out his knife, the thumb is already pressed against the knife's opening mechanism. That way there is no danger presented in grasping an open knife. The

Decisions, decisions: trouser clip on the blade holder ("tip down carry") or on the handle end ("tip up carry") of the folding knife.

■ **Cordura case from Blackhawk. As with all cases of this design, tearing it open produces an undesirable noise during tactical operations.**

■ **Knife holsters made out of Kydex allow quick access without first having to open up a folder. Pictured here is a holster made by sheath manufacturer Werner Lüttecken.**

catchline serves no purpose in helping to pull it out. A final decision cannot be made as to which of the two clip positions is better, since each has its advantages and disadvantages. As with all tactical carrying methods, the decision should be made according to what constitutes an instinctive grip and secure handling for the individual. On the other hand, it is indisputable that the clip should be mounted as far outside as possible so that the knife only peeks out of the pocket a bit and is not noticeable. From a tactical standpoint, a knife can be attached with a clip to every imaginable place on clothing or equipment. If the knife has no available clip, knifemaker Allen Elishewitz offers an interesting solution: he designed an open Cordura case with a clip, thereby achieving the same effect.

Whoever does not have a clip for his knife or simply feels it is uncomfortable has to carry his knife in a case. Whether it is made of leather or Cordura, it should be able to be carried both vertically and horizontally. With many cases, the loops can also be opened and closed with Velcro fasteners, which again increases their tactical utility. This way the case can be attached to a tactical belt or leg belt, combat vest or backpack. Ultimately, the way someone attaches his case depends on the responsibilities of his mission, what kind of equipment he has and the ability to grab it instinctively. Nothing could be worse than the user having to think about where his knife is located on his body, thereby losing valuable reaction time. This principle applies both to folding knives and to fixed-blade knives.

On the other hand, with most tactical cases the use of Velcro fasteners is critical. Especially in the still of the night or in similar situations, the scratching sound of a Velcro fastener can betray both man and mission. For example, if special police forces find themselves in the immediate proximity of one or more criminals who are unaware of their presence, opening a Velcro fastener is prohibited. The tactically savvy and cautious specialist knows all about this problem. However, the great advantage of the Velcro closure is that it reliably protects against the loss of the knife. The closure is very tight even if, in haste, it has not been pressed onto the entire Velcro fastener. Furthermore, repairs can usually be easily performed with needle and thread.

With traditional push-button or modern synthetic pin closures, there are fewer problems with noisy openings. Pin closures offer the greatest security, because they stop the case from being unintentionally opened when the owner is hanging from branches, a safety belt, or other unforeseeable obstacles.

The use of folding knife holsters is practical. This is an open carrying device that allows the user to pull out his knife without wasting valuable time opening up the blade. These holsters are available in leather as well as Kydex. The leather variants can only be carried horizontally on the belt, while most Kydex models can also be carried vertically upside-down on a string around the neck or on a chest belt. While moisture and constant use can compromise the secure position of a knife in a leather holster, Kydex holsters keep their shape. The disadvantage of both types is that they are usually made specifically for one model, and so they cannot be used for every kind of folding knife.

Blackhawk and Eagle offer interesting Cordura combination cases for folding knives and flashlights, i.e., multifunction tools.

Fixed-Blade Knives

This chapter deals principally with the unconcealed carrying of knives and sheath systems. While previously the unconventional carrying of fixed-blade knives was purely a question of improvisation, modern tactical knife sheaths offer a number of attachment devices with which the user can place his knife exactly where it is most sensible for himself and the tasks at hand.

With unconcealed carrying systems, attaching the knife to the upper thigh has become popular. This development stems from fastening pistols and magazines to the thigh. The pioneers in this field are the British anti-terrorism specialists, the Special Air Services, who made this method of carrying weapons and equipment standard practice as early as the late 1970s and found a corresponding manufacturer in Len Dixon & Son. Fastening the sheath low on the thigh has several advantages. First, the knife can be easily pulled out despite its long blade, without having to bend the arm too much. Second, the knife is located out of the reach of other pieces of equipment that could come into contact with a knife worn in the belt, bulletproof vests, combat vests, backpack straps, or parachutes.

The easiest way to fasten a sheath to the upper thigh is with a leather or nylon cord. Unfortunately, the sheath hardly ever stays in the intended place during running or climbing. If the knife is long and heavy, the inevitable result is that it dangles in an irritating way. Modern tactical sheaths that are attached by one wide or two smaller belts are much more effective by today's standards. An adjustable belt determines how low the sheath sits on the thigh. Of course, if the user's personal equipment

■ **Left: S & S Enterprises' "EOD-Mod. 02" offers the most comfortable method for carrying large knives (knife: "Walter Brend Mod. 5").**

■ **Below: In the special forces, attaching the sheath to the thigh belt of the pistol holster has become standard. Pictured is the "TK16-MV" from knife manufacturer Klötzli.**

includes a pistol holster or a magazine pouch, the knife can be attached with the belt provided. However, it should be ensured that the sheath fits properly into the belt.

Alternative possibilities for attaching the knife to the body are the lower leg, the upper arm, and the lower arm. Usually at least two belts are needed for that. These should be somewhat flexible so that the limbs do not get cut into too tightly with muscular contractions. As has been mentioned many times before, carrying a knife on the belt with the handle down has been one of the habits and quirks of many military special forces since the days of the Vietnam War. There are three reasons for this practice:

1. It gets least in the way of most other equipment when positioned there.

2. The hand only has to travel a short distance to reach the knife. Moreover, it is at an optimal angle.

3. In an emergency, the knife can also be reached with the opposite hand.

Of course, the knife can also be attached in the same way to a combat vest, as long as there is a free surface on the chest. If the vest is made according to the variable or individual equipment, there is generally no problem. Here, too, the SAS was in the forefront. Press photos from the early 1980s show English elite soldiers with "AEK" cutting knives in sewn-on shoulder sheaths. The clear disadvantage of this carrying method is that each time the uniform is put aside, the knife is no longer within reach. For example, if orders are changed, it has to be possible to move the sheath from one place to another without a great deal of effort. Thus, the sheath system and other equipment should be well coordinated with each other and allow for different carrying methods.

Besides the carrying method, the security of the knife plays an important role. With most tactical sheaths, a two-fold security system is used that secures the knife against loss under any circumstance during parachuting or rappelling. According to German aviation law, a knife that is attached to a paratrooper is an external weight and must be secured as such. With most tactical sheaths, this securing device consists of an additional buckle or a rubber ring. Placed on the back of the sheath, this is supposed to keep the handle as close to the body as possible. Once the landing site has been reached, this secondary securing device must be opened.

■ **Classic carrying method—on the backpack with the handle upside down. (Knife: "P. J. Peltonen")**

With primary securing devices, two systems have become popular besides the Kydex system described on page 169: the handle clasp and the hilt clasp. The traditional handle clasp is the older system. From a purely technical standpoint, it should occur in the area of the hilt. In this way the hand is able to grab the handle and open the clasp with the index finger or thumb. This system is especially recommended with dagger blades, since there is only a slight danger of damaging the opened clasp through the sheath. A newer, but much more popular, method is the hilt clasp. This usually runs diagonally over the hilt. The advantages are: (1) The entire length of the handle can be grasped with the hand; and (2) the belt loop is more flexible and makes the entire system more comfortable to carry. However, owners of single-edged knives should take care to fasten the clasp on the back side of the blade to avoid damaging it. One way of fixing the clasp is to "thumb snap." This has the advantage of allowing the user to grab and open it in one sweeping motion. In order for the snap to open easily, a lever-like extension is used, usually a thin steel plate. Because of the increased use of Kydex sheaths, this system is losing acceptance. This method of securing knives became popular with Gerber's boot knives. It remains to be seen whether the mechanical locking systems, which are integral components of synthetic sheaths, can be successfully used with gloves.

■ **Right: This tactical vest from Blackhawk, with a modified attachment pocket, allows a knife to be carried in a variety of ways (even upside down).**

On many leather and Cordura sheaths, there is an additional small pocket on the front. This can be filled with sharpening tools, small flashlights or multifunction tools, which again increases the value of the system as a whole. However, the user should be aware of the added weight.

As with handguns in the special forces, knives can (and should) be additionally secured by means of a spiral cord. For one thing, the knife will not get lost if it happens to slip out of the hand; for another, it will not endanger anyone who happens to be in the direction of the falling knife. With the British "AEK" model, a simple nylon cord serves to secure the knife, and when it is not being used, it can be neatly rolled up in a specially designed compartment. Spiral cords are offered by Blackhawk and Nowar, among along with other manufacturers.

Optional Sheaths and Carrying Accessories

Anyone who owns a good knife, but is unsatisfied with its carrying possibilities or how comfortable it is to carry, can equip it with optional accessories. Nowar, for example, tailor-made a shoulder holster system especially for the Böker "A-F" knife's Kydex sheaths, but it can also be used with sheaths for other models and manufacturers. This system, which can be carried on the right or the left, offers a high level of comfort that is achieved by providing an individual fit for all kinds of belts. For open tactical use, the sturdier Cordura edition is recommended.

Those who wish to carry their knives in various angles on belts, backpacks or other equipment should take a look at the extremely durable TEK-LOK system, made out of fiberglass-strengthened synthetic material and developed by Bob Terzuola and Blade-Tech. It works best with a Kydex sheath, but leather and Cordura sheaths can also be mounted on it to a certain extent, depending on whether they are stable enough and have places where holes can be bored. The front of this practical system can be opened so that the TEK-LOK can also be fastened to other equipment. In the author's opinion, this is perhaps the most efficient sheath accessory ever developed.

■ The "LSACS-Mod. 05" sheath system by S&S Enterprises for knifemaker Harold Carson's model "U-2."

Photo: S & S Enterprises/Livingston

At this time, Blackhawk and Eagle offer the best Cordura sheaths with interiors enhanced by synthetic materials for various knife models. There is hardly any difference in their designs or how they are produced. The large front pocket is excellently suited for stowing multifunction tools. The sheath can be carried either directly on a belt loop or lower on the thigh, using an adaptation system. A clasp fixes the sheath directly onto the relatively wide leg belt, which stops the sheath from turning on the thigh. A rubber ring inside the belt reinforces this anti-motion effect. Ring loops offer additional attachment possibilities. Both manufacturers offer their models in standard black and olive green. Camouflage models are also available by special order. S&S Enterprises offers a design that combines the advantages of Kydex and Cordura. The outer shell consists of Cordura with a front clasp, and diverse pieces of equipment can be stored in various large pockets. A Kydex sheath is firmly attached inside, which is shaped in typical fashion around the hilt and holds the knife without means of a clasp. True, these sheaths are only available for a small number of models. But it is also possible to have them individually made. The most extravagant sheath system for the thigh is made by S&S Enterprises under the name "LSACS" (Land Sea Air Carry System). As the name suggests, it is suitable for land and sea missions as well as for parachuting. This system, containing a number of large pockets that are connected to the sheath as a single unit, offers ample room to store different pieces of equipment.

If someone prefers to store his knife in a pure Kydex sheath and money is no object, he can have one individually made by American Kydex specialists Blade-Tech or Scott Hendrix. Not quite as custom-made, but certainly cheaper, is EdgeWorks' Kydex sheath system created for knives with blades up to 18 cm long.

■ **Nowar's shoulder carrying system was developed especially for Böker's "A-F" Kydex sheaths, but fits models by other manufacturers.**

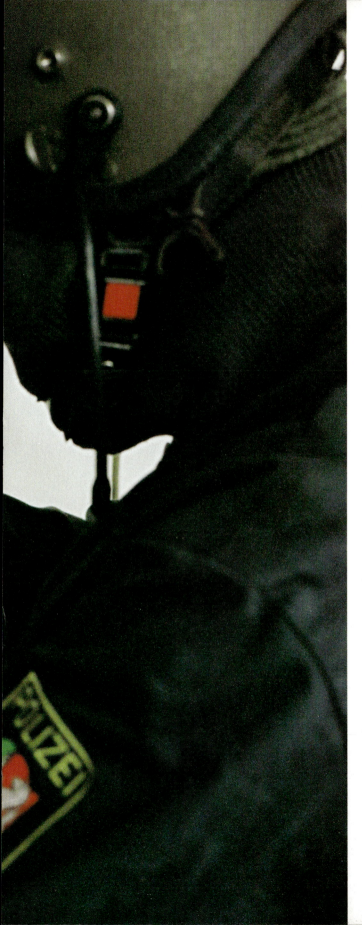

Multifunction Tools in Tactical Deployment

The history of multifunction tools can be traced back to WWII. An "escape knife" was issued to British pilots as well as members of the secret service, the SOE, and its American counterpart, the OSS. The Sheffield firm Joseph Rodgers & Sons built it after a design dating back to Victorian times. The purpose of this tactical tool was to give prisoners of war the chance to escape. The most important component was the pliers, which allowed barbed-wire fences to be cut through. So that the enemy wouldn't find the tool on the prisoner's person, the little escape knife was usually hidden somewhere in his clothing.

In 1975 the old idea of a multifunction tool was revived. Tim Leatherman, an American who was taking an adventure trip through Europe, was continually confronted with various situations in which he needed different tools. His old pocket knife wasn't up to the challenge. He took some notes and upon his return to the United

■ **An SEK officer gains access to a fuse box with his multifunction tool.**
Photo: Thomas Ruhl

States he developed a tool that went into production in 1983, after many prototypes and hundreds of tests. Although it was developed as a tool for everyone, the police and military quickly recognized its value for tactical use. The "Pocket Survival Tool" ("PST") was, after Joseph Rodgers & Sons' "Escape Knife," one of the first multifunction tools that was officially adopted into the supplies of Western armies. The official NATO supply number for the PST is 5120-99-786-5369. Besides well-known military elite groups like the American Navy SEALs and the British Royal Marines, German SEKs use it as well. Indeed, the multifunction tool has superseded the knife in the special police forces to the greatest possible extent, yet it cannot be properly described as its successor. True, the tactical value of the multifunction tool is many times greater, but the two pieces of equipment are not comparable. With the little "tool box," the individual can carry out tasks for which earlier either a materials vest had to be carried or specifically requested logistical forces had to be used. The approach of the logistical forces to the site would generally be carried out with tactical difficulties and delays. The duties of these forces have certainly not abated in any way, but they have shifted to more difficult and expensive areas of responsibility. The best tool is of no use if it isn't on one's person when it is needed, and momentous situations often fall apart because of small things.

The tactical uses of multifunction tools are highly diverse and can hardly be described in their entirety. Here are just a few examples: When laying demolition explosives, wire cutters and strippers are indispensable. The same goes for removing explosives. With screwdrivers, which are usually available in different sizes, hinges on doors and windows can be unscrewed. The wire cutter on the head of the pliers serves equally well for cutting through handcuffs, which as a rule are enormously resistant. Depending on how the tool is equipped, saws, bottle openers and can openers render invaluable service in preparing food during field operations. The list could go on and on.

Just as with tactical knives, the surfaces of multifunction tools should not be reflective. It would be fatal for a simple reflection of light to betray and doom a mission. So most manufacturers offer versions in black for the special forces. Unfortunately, experience has shown that these surface coatings are often very delicate. However, just as with firearms, the coating generally comes off a little on the most stressed areas and the larger surfaces stay black, so it doesn't really matter.

In general, little attention is paid to the standard mounted grommets for catch lines, even though these can be enormously important on a mission. In some circumstances, losing one's tool can spell the difference between life and death.

Just as extensive as the methods in which the multifunction tool can be used is the palette of available models. Nearly every American knife manufacturer has introduced its own model onto the market. Even the Swiss firm Victorinox has added a high-quality multifunction tool to the selection. Many "multis," unfortunately, are difficult if not impossible to handle. It must be supposed that some manufacturers simply want to distinguish their products from Leatherman's. The first generation of multifunction tools unfortunately did not offer any useful locking mechanisms. In particular, using the blade posed a latent risk of injury. The second generation of multifunction tools did include a standard locking mechanism. Nevertheless, the owners of certain models were still vulnerable to unpleasant experiences. For example, the firm grip of the pliers is not exactly a delight if the gripping edges press into the fingers and palm. Leatherman has learned a lesson from these kinds of experiences and changed the handle on his "Wave" model accordingly. All the same, the old models "PST" and "Super Tool" (also available in black) remain then as now the most widely used multifunction tool among the special forces. The accompanying leather cases are still very compact, to be sure, but they look rather unsightly after a few weeks' use. Alternatively, the manufacturer offers a Cordura case with a Velcro fastener. But

■ **Tactical multifunction tools in special black editions. Top row: Leatherman's "Super Tool" and Victorinox's "Swiss Tool." Bottom row: Leatherman's "Pocket Survival Tool" and Gerber's "D.E.T."**

Photo: Bernd Schlemper/Andreas Jatridis

for obvious reasons, in various tactical situations the use of a Velcro fastener is exceedingly critical.

Leatherman's biggest competitor is certainly Gerber. The greatest advantage of its multifunction tool is the fact that the pliers can be opened with one hand. With a flick of the wrist, the pliers flip out and lock into position. Like Leatherman, Gerber also offers two models that are intended for tactical use (i.e. were developed especially for that purpose): the black "Multilock" and the "D.E.T." ("Demolition Explosive Technician"). The latter is equipped with tools that can be used with explosives. Among these is a special set of pliers for preparing detonation devices and a punch ("C-4 Punch") for boring holes for detonation capsules in plastic explosives. Both models come standard with a very resilient Cordura case.

The Victorinox firm makes a black model of its "Swiss Tool" especially for

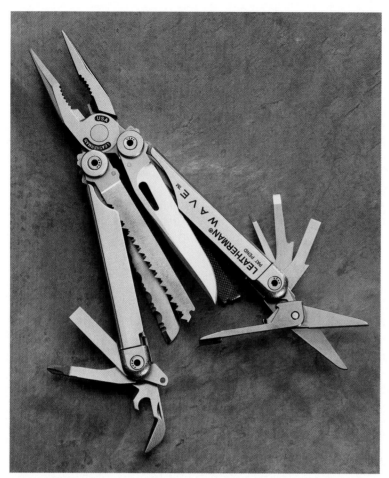

■ According to Tim Leatherman, the "Wave" model has outstripped the "Super Tool" in popularity among the special forces.

the Norwegian army (NATO supply number 5110-25-147-5018). A fourth manufacturer is the firm SOG Specialty Knives with its models "Power Plier" and "Para Tool" models, both of which are also available with a black coating.

The tactical field cannot be imagined without multifunction tools, but each user should be clearly aware of their limitations. In particular, *in no case* in a tactical situation do they replace knives, which one can grab for in an emergency and cut oneself free from a rope or parachute with lightening lightning speed. As a rule, both hands are needed to open first the pliers and then the knife. And if tactical gloves are being worn, the whole thing becomes even more complicated. It is true that with the "Wave," Leatherman tries to solve the problem by placing a blade on the outside that can be used one-handed, but with gloves it is still a problem. With all multifunction tools, the risk of injury under enormous stress cannot be ruled out because, of course, the handles feature no hand protection device that could stop the hand from slipping onto the blade. Because there is no insulation, the multifunction tool also cannot be used to work on electrical lines. As a matter of principle, only special tools should be used in such cases.

TACTICAL KNIVES

In short, multifunction tools are by all means a sensible complement to tactical knives, but are not a substitute for them, even if authorities sometimes want to claim that they are.

House Call at Dawn, or "Let Sleeping Dogs Lie:" Why a multifunction tool is no substitute for a knife

Certainly nothing out of the ordinary for the police force of a large city: An armed and dangerous pimp who is wanted for murder, robbery and other "trifles" is to be arrested at his hideout.

While the residents of this contemplative quarter of the city are still fast asleep at 5:00 in the morning, the front door on the second floor of a renovated old building splinters and the shout "Police, don't move!" rends the musty air of the two-room apartment.

SEK forces in protective gear are invading the first room, weapons ready to fire, when out of the bedroom at the end of the hall emerges an obviously bad-tempered but well-fed pit bull terrier that immediately attacks.

A gunshot from one of the police officers aborts the attempt right away, and the badly injured animal flees back into the bed of his ill-reputed master and a scantily clad woman!

For the six-foot-tall murder suspect, the revolver in the night table is no longer an issue options in view of the SEK officers in his bedroom and the blood-covered dog in his bed. White as a sheet and trembling, he is handcuffed. His companion is given over to the custody of a policewoman, and an emergency physician treats the suspect for shock. In light of the seriously wounded dog's position and the number of people in the vicinity, the aggressive animal, whose gunshot wounds leave him no chance of survival, is dispatched on the spot with the squad leader's Gerber "Mark II" and put out of his misery.

A speedy search of the room is begun with no threat to officers or innocent bystanders from the injured dog or the additional use of firearms.

Incidentally, the officer had experience hunting and trapping animals with knives. For this purpose the blade of a tactical knife or a hunting knife proved to be the best thing. Multifunction tools are not appropriate for such uses—unless in an unforeseeable emergency.

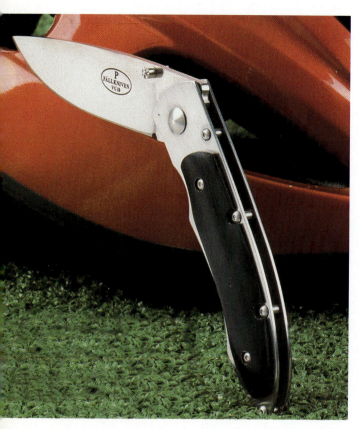

Got Game? Go Tactical!

Tactical and sporting knives mesh to address the outdoors needs of cutlery enthusiasts

By Joe Kertzman
Managing Editor, *Blade* Magazine

■ The Falkniven Model P frame-lock folder comes with a Cordura® belt pouch for ease of carry in such sporting situations as mountain biking. A thumb stud makes the VG-10 blade easily accessible, and the Micarta® handle is durable and light-weight.

Think of it as the meshing of tacticals and sporting folders or fixed blades. Consider it a new incarnation of knife. It's the all-around player, the tactical extremist, a kayaker's dream, the mountain climber's must-have, the snowboarder's saving grace, a blade that better be there when the chips are down. Isn't that how tacticals are built anyway?

This is a subject that excites Paul Gillespie of Columbia River Knife & Tool. It's why he's in the knife business—to build knives that cross traditional blade boundaries. "There is a relatively new industry called 'outdoor retailing.' It's a place where you go if you want to buy a mountain bike, a superior backpack or climbing gear. It's for the young person today who doesn't necessarily hunt or fish, but who's into the 'non-blood sports,'" Gillespie explains.

"The [CRKT] Crawford/Kasper is one of the best-selling knives in that industry," he claims, "but as recent as five years ago, you would never have thought that type of tactical folder would be sold in such a retail sporting environment. Tacticals are built to perform, and someone hanging off a rock needs a knife that will perform."

Gillespie suggests, "Probably the first company that made inroads into outdoor-retailing-type stores, beyond the makers of Swiss Army knives, was Spyderco. There was a time when Spyderco folders were nearly the only one-hand-opening knives."

Before discussing the meshing of tactical fixed blades or folders with sporting-type knives, Spyderco's Sal Glesser redefines the term "tactical" as it applies to knives. "We at Spyderco feel we created tactical folders, but not in terms of combat," Glesser notes. "A strategic plan is a long-term plan. A tactical plan is here and now. Tactical folders were created for the here and now, for accessing an edged tool quickly. That's where the Spyderco hole in the blade came in handy.

"If a horse rider's leg is tangled in rope, he needs to access his knife now," Glesser expounds. "If a knife gets you out of trouble, it's a tactical knife, whether you're climbing a mountain or caught in a fish net. Tactical folders were not designed for combat. You could come up with a dozen situations that are sporting/tactical situations, and a tactical-type knife is probably most important in extreme sports scenarios."

In designing a knife for sporting/tactical purposes, Glesser pinpoints weight consciousness as crucial, a one-hand-opening device for folding knives as extremely important, and reliability as critical. "A tactical blade is a sharp point that cuts well," he says. "It doesn't matter the blade shape. You're back to performance regardless of shape."

■ **Among other features, the Columbia River Knife & Tool M1 has a wide "paddle clip" that can be carried in any position and attached to almost all gear. The M1 is designed by Greg Lightfoot.**

Samurai Mountain Man?

"The guy in the bush pays more attention to the swell in the handle and the overall knife ergonomics. Performance is important. Extreme sportsmen aren't worried about meeting bad guys on the mountain," Glesser reasons. "The traditional sporty aspects of knives used to be limited to hunting blades. Now people want sea-kayaking knives."

When asked what the ideal blade shape for the extreme sportsman would be if there was one, Glesser answers, "no more than necessary and no less than perfect, just like in nature. It doesn't matter if the blade is shaped like a leaf, a claw or a tooth.

"We've always sold the Ladybug models to mountain climbers who wear them strung from lanyards around their necks," Glesser notes. "We've sold lightweight, high-performance knives, like the Delica, into the outdoor retailing industry for 10-12 years. I'm always making knives lighter, stronger and more durable."

The Delica and Ladybug lockback folders have both been in the Spyderco line since 1990, and each is similarly shaped, with one-hand-opening holes in serrated blades, and integral lanyard holes at the butts of the handles. The Ladybug is 2 1/2 inches closed and meant to be attached to a key ring, or carried in a pocket or purse. The Delica features a pocket clip and is 4 inches closed.

Columbia River Knife & Tool debuted the Lightfoot M1 at the 2003 S.H.O.T. (Shooting Hunting Outdoor Trade) Show. It features a wide, full-bellied, titanium-nitride-coated AUS-8 blade. A dimpled and injection-molded Zytel® handle completes an all-black look. Described as a "refined-tanto," the blade is semi-serrated and employs a thumb stud, a Kit Carson-designed Flipper for assisted opening, and a LAWKS (Lake And Walker Knife Safety) to prevent accidental disengagement of the locking liner.

■ **The melding of tactical and sporting features on one knife is no more evident than with the Browning Model 6012 Barracuda. A locking-liner folder, it show-cases a 3 1/2-inch black, drop-point AUS-8A blade with a thumb stud.**

"The M1 has a very wide clip we call a 'paddle clip' that mounts in four positions on the knife," Gillespie details. "It can be carried in any position and attached to almost all gear. Though it's not a huge knife, the heavy, compact build is suited for just about anything you want to use a knife for while rock climbing, mountain biking, kayaking, river rafting, backpacking, or whatever."

Knifemaker Ken Onion says the problem with most hunting knives in the past is that they were too job specific and not suited for overall utility, or built with ultra-toughness in mind. "People look at tacticals and see durability," Onion opines. "By melding the best features of tacticals and utility hunters together, you create a more homogenous, multi-purpose knife."

"Ergo-Tech," Not Tactical

"That's where the knife industry is going—to undefined blade shapes," Onion predicts. "The nice thing about melding tacticals with sporting knives is that you end up with less massive, angular knives and more ergonomic, comfortable and fluid knives that serve more than one purpose. I prefer to call them 'ergo-tech,' not tactical."

Onion also sees and senses more textured, rather than smooth, knife handles in the sporting/tactical genre and, as noted, undefined blade shapes, but made up of state-of-the-art steels that don't have to be sharpened as often. Knife carry options are also increasing, he says.

"That's the beauty of multi-carry rigs. You can

attach a knife to your backpack, carry it on your hip or in the small of your back, clip it inside or outside of pants pockets, or sling it around your neck or under your arm," Onion determines. "There is no defined specific carry place, so the customer has more options.

"I think people are getting more adventurous and, realistically, when the chips are down and you're in the woods with only a few tools, your best chance of survival is a knife," he adds. "We're in an era now when more people want to buy a fixed blade. It's the best bang for the buck and more multi-purpose and multi-tasking than folders."

One such fixed example is the Kershaw Vertigo, designed by Onion with a 4-inch AUS-8A blade, a textured-Polyamide™ handle and a Kydex® sheath that mounts on a belt in several positions.

"Kershaw came out with the Echo, a knife I designed based around hunting first and utility second," Onion says. "People expressed interest in a knife with a more distinct point and a straighter blade bevel, not as pronounced of a recurve along the edge. Tacticals took the knife industry by storm 10 years ago. This is a natural progression."

The melding of tactical and sporting features on one knife is no more evident than with the Browning Model 6012 Barracuda. Rising above the surface of the camouflage-Zytel® handle are black-Kraton® circles for positive hand purchase. A locking-liner folder, it showcases a 3 1/2-inch, black, drop-point AUS-8A blade with a thumb stud.

Non-Militaristic Knives

"Unless they have a hard, military appearance, tacticals have always looked sporty to me," remarks knifemaker Fred Carter. "I am trying hard to make my folders look both sporty and tactical to appeal to a wider market. In some cases, I have tried to achieve a military look but, for me, the flowing design elements always creep into the shape. I just don't like the clunky look.

"With the hi-tech materials available, like G-10, carbon fiber and aircraft aluminum, the weight is kept down and the strength of these knives is incredible," Carter adds. "The fact that most can be operated with one hand is also a positive for the extreme sportsman, and many have a good gripping surface, which is also appealing to field users."

The aircraft-aluminum handle of the Carter-designed M4-K folder from United Cutlery showcases a Magna-Grip™, similar to a sandpaper- or roofing-paper-type texture. It is complemented by a 3 3/8-inch, bead-blasted, 440 stainless steel blade, a button lock and a pocket clip.

Two folders with raised handle surfaces are the Buck Folding Alpha Hunter and the Fallkniven Model P, each with stainless-steel frames and handle overlays. The Alpha Hunter is a locking-liner folder with a choice of rosewood or rubber handle overlays, a 3 1/2-inch, drop-point ATS-34 blade and a Cordura® sheath. MSRP: $70-$104, depending on materials.

The Fallkniven Model P is a frame-lock folder featuring a 3 1/8-inch VG-10 blade, also a drop point, a 420J2 handle frame and a black-Micarta® grip.

"I don't know that most of these knives are specifically designed for climbing, mountain biking or whitewater rafting. We at CRKT don't do it, not specifically for that trade," Gillespie says. "It's just that the Crawford/Kasper will work equally as well in extreme sporting situations as it will in Afghanistan. The outdoor sporting business has exploded in the last five years. Now, it's a fairly saucy industry."

This report first appeared in the June 2003 issue of *Blade* magazine.

■ **Top: Meshing the design elements of sporting folders or fixed blades with those of tacticals is easier than ever, with hi-tech materials such as G-10, carbon fiber and aircraft aluminum. The aircraft-aluminum handle of the Fred Carter-designed M4-K folder from United Cutlery showcases a Magna-Grip™, similar to a sandpaper- or roofing-paper-type texture. It is complemented by a 3 3/8-inch, bead-blasted, 440 stainless steel blade, a button lock and a pocket clip. Bottom: A locking-liner folder, the Buck Alpha Hunter is delivered with a stainless-steel handle frame and a choice of rosewood or rubber overlays, a 3 1/2-inch, drop-point ATS-34 blade and a Cordura® sheath.**

Final Thoughts

Looking at the development of tactical knives, one might be tempted to say that there probably isn't anything more to be done. Quite the contrary! Innovations are fundamentally obscure. In particular, the quality of steel in terms of cutting ability and resistance to corrosion is continually increasing. High-tech materials like titanium, ceramic and synthetic materials have not been able to outdo steel as a blade material; however, in certain areas they succeed as valuable support materials.

Thanks to highly precise CNC manufacturing methods, more and more modern and high-qualityhigh quality locking systems have been developed for flick flick-blade knives. Because of advisors from the field of special forces, tactical knife design is becoming increasingly tailored to the needs and demands of the jobs they are designed for. In this regard, more and more attention is being paid to carrying systems and modern materials like Kydex and Cordura. It would be presumptuous to say that developments are basically at a standstill.

■ **The young** *Kommando Spezialkräfte* **of the** *Bundeswehr* **recognized the importance of knives in special operations.**
Photo: BmVg

Even if over the centuries the knife has lost some of its importance, it is still necessary in many areas of daily life. Even the classic combat knife has maintained its importance for military use, as shown by the example of the *Bundeswehr*'s "Kommando Spezialkräfte." In spite of brilliant technological developments in the arms sector, the knife is, as it has been for decades, the ultimate means of triumphing over an opponent in hand-to-hand combat.

In Germany, the knife has long ago disappeared from the general equipment of the police, mainly for political reasons. Only in the national and state special forces and customs are knives still carried. But even there knives are employed primarily as tools, and as weapons only in an extreme emergency.

Weapon or tool, the tactical knife continues to evolve. There will be enough new developments in the coming years that will make writing about them worthwhile.

About the Author

Only a few people are lucky enough to be able to combine their hobby with their profession. Dietmar Pohl, who was born in 1966, is one of these few people. Collecting knives has been his great passion for years. It began in the 1980s with knives from films, and later expanded into the areas of combat and technical knives. Since receiving his degree in economics in 1994 at the Bergischen Universität Wuppertal, where he majored in marketing, he has been employed as director of marketing at the Solingen knife manufacturer Heinr. Böker Baumwerk. His field of activity is not limited merely to marketing products through Magnum knife catalogs, but calls upon his qualities as a knife designer who, as a passionate knife aficionado, has a good feeling for innovative forms, functions, and small details. Hence, the design of the annual Magnum Collection series has been drafted by himhe has drafted the design of the annual Magnum Collection series since 1995. He has also designed various tactical knives, including "Speedlock" and "Gemini,", and co-designed the "Orca." In addition, he was substantially involved in the development of knives for the arms manufacturers Walther and Heckler & Koch.

■ The author (right) together with a member of the Woodbridge, New Jersey SWAT team during tactical submachine gun training in Sterling, Virginia.

In rendering his ideas and designs in the field of tactical knives, Dietmar Pohl focuses primarily on functionality and the needs of professional users in the area of special forces. In order to broaden his knowledge, he maintains close contact with special forces in Germany and the U.S.A.

As a sideline, Dietmar Pohl writes for such trade journals as *VISIER*, *Caliber*, *Waffenmarkt Intern* and *Messer Magazin*. These articles have covered such topics as knives from films and tactical knives and their carrying systems. In the spring of 2001, together with the Deutsches Klingenmuseum in Solingen, he organized the first worldwide exhibition on the topic of knives in films.

Dietmar Pohl is a member of the following organizations:
Honorary member of the American Knifemaker's Guild since 1988
Founding member of the American Bladesmith Society since 1994
Member of the Deutsche Messermacher-Gilde since 1996

Essential Internet Sites Devoted to Tactical Knives and Accessories

Organizations, Publications and Other Resources

American Bladesmith Society
www.bladesmith.com
Educational and professional organization

American Knife & Tool Institute
www.akti.org
Dedicated to promoting pro-knife education and legislation

Blade Magazine
www.blademag.com
From Krause Publications. Published monthly

Cutting Edge Training
www.cuttingedgetraining.com
Offers knife training for law enforcement officers

Knifemakers' Guild
www.kmg.org
Professional organization for custom knifemakers

Military Knives
www.militaryknives.org
Online photo gallery of collectible military knives

Randall Knife Society
www.randallknifesociety.com
Organization for enthusiasts and collectors of Randall knives

Tactical Knives Magazine
www.tacticalknives.com
From Harris Outdoor Group. Published six times per year.

U.S. Military Knives
www.usmilitaryknives.com
Information on U.S. military knives, bayonets and machetes

Manufacturers

Al Mar Knives
www.almarknives.com

Benchmade Knife Co.
www.benchmade.com

Beretta USA Corp.
www.beretta.com

Boker USA Inc.
www.BokerUSA.com

Busse Combat Knife Co.
www.combatknives.com

CAS Iberia Inc.
www.casiberia.com

Camillus Cutlery Co.
www.camillusknives.com

Chris Reeve Knives
www.chrisreeve.com

Cold Steel Inc.
www.coldsteel.com

Columbia River Knife & Tool
www.crkt.com

Pat Crawford Knives
www.crawfordknives.com

Emerson Knives Inc.
www.emersonknives.com

Fallkniven AB
www.fallkniven.com

Gerber Legendary Blades
www.gerberblades.com

GT Knives
www.gtknives.com

Gutmann Cutlery Inc.
www.gutmanncutlery.com

KA-BAR Knives Inc.
www.ka-bar.com

Katz Knives Inc.
www.katzknives.com

Kershaw Knives
www.kershawknives.com

Klotzli
www.klotzli.com

Knifeware Inc.
www.knifeware.com

Leatherman Tool Group Inc.
www.leatherman.com

Meyerco USA
www.meyercousa.com

Microtech
www.microtechknives.com

Mission Knives & Tools Inc.
www.missionknives.com

Ontario Knife Co.
www.ontarioknife.com

Randall Made Knives
www.randallknives.com

SOG Specialty Knives
www.sogknives.com

Spyderco Inc.
www.spyderco.com

Taylor Cutlery
www.taylorcutlery.com

TiNives
www.tinives.com

Online Retailers

2 The Hilt
www.2thehilt.com

Beck's Cutlery
www.beckscutlery.com

Best Knives
www.bestknives.com

Blackhawk Industries
www.blackhawkindustries.com

Bladeshack Knives
www.bladeshack.com

Knife Center of the Internet
www.knifecenter.com

One Stop Knife Shop
www.1SKS.com

Pete's Tactical Knives
www.petestacticalknives.com

R&S Tactical Gear
www.rstacticalgear.com

Sharper Things
www.sharperthings.com

Wolf Den Knives
www.wolfdenknives.com